Peter Coffield and Swoosie Kurtz in a scene from the Hartman Theatre production of "The Middle Ages." Set designed by John Lee Beatty.

THE
MIDDLE AGES

A COMEDY IN TWO ACTS
BY A.R. GURNEY

★

DRAMATISTS
PLAY SERVICE
INC.

THE MIDDLE AGES was first produced at the Mark Taper Forum Lab in January, 1977, with the following cast:

```
BARNEY ..............................Cliff de Young
ELEANOR..............................Kitty Winn
CHARLES .............................Keene Curtis
MYRA ................................Toni Lamonde
```

It was directed by Gordon Hunt.

It opened for a three week run at the Hartman Theatre in Stamford, Connecticut, in January, 1978, with the following cast:

```
BARNEY ..............................Peter Coffield
ELEANOR .............................Swoosie Kurtz
CHARLES .............................Douglass Watson
MYRA ................................Patricia O'Connell
```

It was directed by Melvin Bernhardt, designed by John Lee Beatty, and lit by Dennis Parichy.

The staging incorporated into this script is primarily from the latter production.

THE MIDDLE AGES was produced off-Broadway in March, 1983, by Alison Clarkson, Stephen Graham, Joan Stein and The Shubert Organization at the Theatre At St. Peter's Church with the following cast:

```
BARNEY ..............................Jack Gilpin
ELEANOR .............................Ann McDonough
CHARLES..............................Andre Gregory
MYRA ................................Jo Henderson
```

Setting by John Lee Beatty
Costumes by David Murin
Lighting by Frances Aronson
Stage Manager: M.A. Howard
The production was directed by David Trainer

Original New York production by the Ark Theatre Company

CAST OF CHARACTERS

BARNEY

ELEANOR

CHARLES, Barney's father

MYRA, Eleanor's mother

The action takes place in the trophy room of a men's club in a large city over a span of time from the mid forties to the late seventies.

The trophy room: Victorian Gothic. Plenty of wood, plenty of leather, plenty of dusty old trophies on shelves. Upstage, a Gothic, mullioned window, with leaded glass, looking out over a gray cityscape. Branches of a tree or shrub intervene.

On the walls, above the wainscotting, are a number of stuffed heads of animals: moose, bear, mountain goat, gazelle; also several racks of guns, fishing rods, along with cases of flies and reels, and mounted game fish. Along shelves, in addition to the trophies, are plaques indicating who killed or caught what, who beat whom, and when. Old wooden tennis racquets, squash racquets, and polo mallets are crossed heraldi-cally and mounted on the wall.

There's a cracked old leather couch, several chairs, and a large oaken table, displaying more trophies and prizes. The effect should be baronial, cluttered, and unused. This is a place where members of the club put things that they've won, or inherited, things they don't know quite what to do with.

Stage Left, a wooden door leads to an old, rarely-used bathroom; Stage Right, larger wooden double doors lead to a panelled hall and the main rooms of the club.

THE MIDDLE AGES

ACT ONE

BEFORE CURTAIN: *The sound of a piano playing a hymn: "Now the Day is Over."*
AT CURTAIN: *Barney stands at the window, back to the audience, looking out. Snow on the branches indicates winter; the light indicates late afternoon. He wears a gray flannel suit, and his sideburns are flecked with gray. After a long moment, the doors on the Right open. The sound of the hymn is heard, louder, from Offstage. Eleanor comes in, wearing a trim black dress, in the style of the late seventies. Barney turns at the noise. Eleanor closes the doors behind her, shutting out the sound Offstage. She is in her forties, lovely, well gotten up. They look at each other for a moment.*

ELEANOR. I knew you'd be in here.
BARNEY. Where else would I be?
ELEANOR. (*Indicating the door.*) Out there. With the rest of us.
BARNEY. Doing what?
ELEANOR. Holding the fort, at least today.
BARNEY. I'll be out when they begin the service. (*He turns back to look out the window. She moves into the room.*)
ELEANOR. Mother sent me to track you down.
BARNEY. She did, did she?
ELEANOR. She wants you to join the family.
BARNEY. She's not *my* mother.
ELEANOR. Well she's mine, Barney, and she's your father's widow, and we should do what she wants on this particular day.
BARNEY. I'll be out when I'm ready, El. (*Pause. She joins him by the window.*)
ELEANOR. She's worried about you, Barney. She thinks you're upset.

5

BARNEY. She's right, for once.

ELEANOR. She thinks you're going to make some kind of speech.

BARNEY. Right again.

ELEANOR. Well she's nervous about that, Barney.

BARNEY. So am I. That's why I'm in here, thinking it out.

ELEANOR. No, but look, the thing is, everyone's pretty exhausted from the church. The feeling is here, here at the club, we should probably boil things down to a bare minimum. Your father would have hated dragging things out. He would have been the first to complain.

BARNEY. So?

ELEANOR. So here, after people arrive, all Mother wants to do is just sing his favorite hymn—

BARNEY. "A Mighty Fortress is Our God."

ELEANOR. I guess so, Barney, I don't know. The point is Billy will play it on the piano, and we'll all *sing* it. And then a few members of the club will get up and make some very brief remarks, and then we'll have a moment of silence, and then—over and out and into the bar. O.K.?

BARNEY. O.K. Got the picture.

ELEANOR. Good. Then I'll tell Mother . . . (*She starts for the door.*)

BARNEY. Tell her I'll be brief. (*Eleanor stops, turns back, takes a deep breath.*)

ELEANOR. Please, Barney.

BARNEY. What's the matter?

ELEANOR. Mother doesn't want you to say anything at all.

BARNEY. Why?

ELEANOR. You know why.

BARNEY. Why can't I say a few words in memory of my own father?

ELEANOR. Because everybody's absolutely terrified, that's why.

BARNEY. Terrified? Of what?

ELEANOR. That you'll say something perfectly ghastly and ruin the whole goddam day!

BARNEY. You think I'd do that?

ELEANOR. Oh, Barney.

BARNEY. You really think I'd do that?

ELEANOR. I think you might. Yes.

BARNEY. You really think I'd fuck up my own father's funeral?

ELEANOR. (*Defiantly.*) I really think you might. Yes.

BARNEY. Oh Christ, El.

ELEANOR. Well you've done it before.

BARNEY. What do you mean? He never *died* before.

ELEANOR. You know what I mean, Barney. Whenever people have gotten together around here, you've done something awful.

BARNEY. All because of you, El.

ELEANOR. (*Coming down from the balcony.*) That's a lie.

BARNEY. (*Following her.*) All because of you.

ELEANOR. That's not true, Barney.

BARNEY. Everything I've done is because of you.

ELEANOR. That is a big, fat *lie,* Barney.

BARNEY. You should have chosen me, El.

ELEANOR. That's enough, please.

BARNEY. Me, instead of my nice straight little brother.

ELEANOR. I said that's enough.

BARNEY. Of course you can still repair the damage.

ELEANOR. Please stop.

BARNEY. I'm still around. Still here. All you need to do is make your move.

ELEANOR. Barney, we are at a *funeral!* Honestly! (*Pause.*) Whatever went on between you and me is over. (*Pause.*) It was all back in the Middle Ages. (*Pause.*) Now. Are you going to make a speech? Or not?

BARNEY. I have things to say. (*He returns to the window.*)

ELEANOR. Well you just plain can't.

BARNEY. Why not?

ELEANOR. Only members can speak.

BARNEY. I'm a member.

ELEANOR. You are not, Barney. You're from out of town.

BARNEY. I am a *permanent* member of this club! I've been trying for thirty years to resign, they've been trying for thirty years to kick me out. It can't be done. It's against some fundamental rule. Once you're born into these things, you're doomed to lifetime membership.

ELEANOR. Not me. I'm not.

BARNEY. Well I am. And so was my father. Hell, this room— here's where we really live.

ELEANOR. Nobody ever comes in here, Barney.

BARNEY. Nobody dares. It's too much. It's the holy of holies, the inner sanctum, the castle keep.

ELEANOR. For you, maybe . . .

BARNEY. For everyone, if they'd just admit it. *(Looks around.)* Look. Here it all is. The weapons, the battle trophies, the sacred chronicles. Pick a book, any book. *(Take a book from the shelf, blows off the dust, reads the title.)* IVANHOE, by Sir Walter Scott. That's us, in three volumes. Heavy armor, extravagant crusades, endless tournaments. And a hero in love with the wrong woman.

ELEANOR. Barney, Mother's waiting.

BARNEY. So what? We're in the sanctuary, El. No one can touch us here. What's out there, anyway? The world, that's all. It doesn't mean much. Because wherever we go, whatever we do, we carry all this with us. On our backs. In our heads. In our blood. Till we die. *(He falls on his knees.)*

ELEANOR. Get up, Barney.

BARNEY. Can't. I'm a prisoner in here. Tried to escape. Couldn't. Here I am. Caught. Doomed. Dead. Hell, bury me in here. Bury the old man. Bury us all. Stack us all up, body on top of body, generation on generation, and let us moulder in here forever. *(Pause.)*

ELEANOR. Is that the speech you've been working on?

BARNEY. I've been working on it all my life. *(He gets up, brushes off his knees.)*

ELEANOR. Well now you've gotten it out of your system, suppose you just come and stand quietly next to Mother, and greet people as they arrive from the cemetery.

BARNEY. Just . . . stand?

ELEANOR. Stand, and even hug people occasionally, and then take Mother to her seat, and sit with her during the service.

BARNEY. Just . . . sit?

ELEANOR. Sit, and hold her hand for once in your life, and keep her from going to pieces.

BARNEY. And you and Billy?

ELEANOR. We'll be sitting on her other side.

BARNEY. Together?

ELEANOR. Together. For your father's sake, Barney. We can all close ranks for that.

BARNEY. Is Billy going to speak?

ELEANOR. Billy?

BARNEY. Billy. My younger brother. Is he going to speak?

ELEANOR. Now Barney—

BARNEY. Yes or no. Is he?

ELEANOR. Mother asked Bill to just say a few words, Barney.

BARNEY. Knew it!

ELEANOR. Oh dear.

BARNEY. Are you going back to him?

ELEANOR. Barney—

BARNEY. After the funeral, are you getting back together?

ELEANOR. Barney, people are beginning to arrive!

BARNEY. (Calling off.) I don't give a SHIT! You're going back to him, aren't you?

ELEANOR. I'm not going back, Barney . . .

BARNEY. Sure you are.

ELEANOR. Here we go.

BARNEY. Damn right here we go! It's the story of my life! You get me all softened up and then you nail me with Billy!

ELEANOR. I think I'll scream!

BARNEY. O.K., baby, here's the thing: (Takes an envelope out of his pocket.) I've got something written down here, and I'm going to read it, all of it, out loud, out there, in front of the assembled multitude. You run and tell your mother that, O.K.? (He sits defiantly on the couch.)

ELEANOR. All right, Barney. I'll tell her that. (She goes to the door, turns.) But before I do, I want to tell you something. Just so you'll know. As soon as we get through this day, as soon as we put your father quietly to rest, I'm through, Barney! I'm through with this family, and this club, and this city! I've spent half my life running back and forth between you, and Billy, and Mother, and your father, and myself, and this is the last day I'm going to do it! (She opens the door; the sounds of a group gathering can be heard.) All of you may be permanent members around here,

9

Barney, but I'm not, and I can't wait to get the HELL out!

BARNEY. Oh Christ, I love you, El.

ELEANOR. Nuts to you, Barney. Just—nuts to you. (*She strides out, leaving the door open. Barney watches her, then goes to stand at the fireplace. The lights fade on the trophy room, except for on him and on the door. The funeral music comes up louder as Charles, Barney's father, appears in the doorway, shadowy and ghostly at first, wearing a dark suit. Barney remains lost in thought.*)

CHARLES. Now, Barney: once again, once again I am obliged to excuse myself from a pleasant occasion in order to cope with my elder son. How many times, Barney, I'm asking you, how many times have I been called out of the office, off the golf course, away from a congenial gathering simply to deal with you. (*He closes the doors behind him. The music can no longer be heard. The lights begin to dim on Barney.*) It seems to me, Barney, that your only interest in this world is to interrupt those few rare moments of social intercourse which men and women have managed to create for themselves in this city. What is the difficulty, Barney? I'd appreciate an answer. (*Barney can no longer be seen. Charles addresses the audience, isolated in light.*) I'd appreciate advice from any quarter. Everything he's done has been disruptive. And it's been that way from the beginning. Why he was even born in the middle of a dinner party. His poor mother had to leave before the dessert. What's more, Doctor Russell tells me the first thing he showed the world was his rear end. And he's continued to show us very little else. When I think of Barney, I think of a whole history of unpleasant incidents. I think of nursemaids in tears because he refused to submit to the ducky chair. I think of cooks packing their bags because he peeked at them in the bathtub. I think of cleaning women huddled in corners while he covered them with a B-B gun. I've tried to civilize him. I send him to kindergarten: the first thing he finds is the fire-alarm. The first thing he writes is a four-letter word. The first thing he draws is the male member. On Winnie-the-Poo. I send him to birthday parties: he pins the tail on the hostess. I send him to summer camp. They send him back. Apparently the only thing he learned was to break wind. At will. And put a match to it. I'm at a loss, my friends. He's a good dancer, but he was expelled from dancing school. For goosing people in the conga line. He's a good hockey player, but he spent half a game in the penalty box. For hiding the puck. In his athletic supporter. He's a good student, but he continually fails history. Why? Because he only will learn about riots, revolutions, and Franklin D. Roosevelt. I am a a loss, my friends. (*Charles goes to the door, opens it: we hear the sound of people singing around the piano, amateurishly but joyously: "O Little Town of Bethlehem." Charles listens for a moment as the lights come up on the room. Barney is standing in the same place, now in a sweater and saddle-shoes, and with the slicked-back hair of the mid-forties. Charles closes the doors and turns to him.*) And now this. This completely outrageous behavior at our first Christmas party since World War Two! How old are you, Barney? (*No response.*) I am asking you a question! How old are you?

BARNEY. (*Quickly joining him D.*) You know how old I am, Dad.

CHARLES. I want to hear it from you.

BARNEY. Sixteen.

CHARLES. Six-teen. Sixteen years old.

BARNEY. You knew that, Dad.

CHARLES. Never mind what I know and what I don't know. Do you consider yourself a man or a boy?

BARNEY. I consider myself—in the middle.

CHARLES. I see. And which do you want to be for the rest of your life?

BARNEY. A man.

CHARLES. And which do you think you were, out there, just now, during the Christmas party?

BARNEY. We were just hacking around, Dad.

CHARLES. Were you a man or a boy out there this afternoon?

BARNEY. All right, I was a boy.

CHARLES. You were a boy, all right. You were a baby. Your little brother, your brother Billy who is only fourteen, is playing the piano out there, and acting twice your age. Now there are families out there who haven't been together since the war. All they wanted to do was come down to this club and gather around the piano and sing some fine old Christmas music. That's all they wanted to do. But would you let them do that? Apparently not. (*Barney shrugs.*) My friends have suggested you miss your mother.

BARNEY. I hardly remember her, Dad.

CHARLES. I miss her.

BARNEY. I know you do, Dad.

CHARLES. Sometimes I miss her so much I almost—lose control.

11

BARNEY. I know, Dad.

CHARLES. But I hold on. I don't run around rooms causing trouble.

BARNEY. I know, Dad.

CHARLES. Then why do *you*?

BARNEY. Maybe I'm just—bad.

CHARLES. Nonsense.

BARNEY. You don't know me, Dad.

CHARLES. I know you perfectly well. And I know it's not too late to repair the damage.

BARNEY. How?

CHARLES. You can apologize. (*Pause.*)

BARNEY. All right. I apologize.

CHARLES. Out there.

BARNEY. Out—?

CHARLES. There.

BARNEY. You mean, make a speech?

CHARLES. That's exactly what I mean.

BARNEY. What about the other boys?

CHARLES. You were the ringleader.

BARNEY. You mean I have to make a speech all by my*self*?

CHARLES. That's what I had to do when I spilled a cocktail on old Mr. Sidway.

BARNEY. But I'm not you, Dad.

CHARLES. You're my older son. And you've got to answer for it. (*He starts for the door.*)

BARNEY. Hey, Dad. Tell you what. Let's have a compromise. O.K.? You go back out there, and I'll go to the movies, O.K.?

CHARLES. I told you this morning. No.

BARNEY. But it's Errol Flynn in *Robin Hood*, Dad. They've brought it back.

CHARLES. Then you've already seen it.

BARNEY. I want to see it *again*, Dad. I could see it a thousand times! I love that movie.

CHARLES. No. I'm sorry. I'm not going to allow my elder son to go to a Hollywood movie in place of a Christmas party. Whose name is on these walls more than any other name?

BARNEY. (*With a sigh.*) Yours.

CHARLES. *Ours.* Who was the first president of this club?

BARNEY. My grandfather.

CHARLES. Your *great*-grandfather. Who—

BARNEY. I *know*, Dad. I know who shot that moose in Wyoming, and who dragged that poor fish out of some lake in the Adirondacks, and whose name is on that cup. (*He indicates cup,* D. L.)

CHARLES. You scoff because you like to be fresh, but someday your name will be on it.

BARNEY. *Why*? Why will it?

CHARLES. Because you're my son. And you can't get away from it. (*Charles opens the door partway. The singing can be heard: "God Rest Ye, Merry Gentlemen."*) All right. Everything seems to have settled down. Now we will go out there, you and I, and I'll announce that you'd like to say a few words.

BARNEY. But what would I say, Dad?

CHARLES. Why you'd simply say you were sorry. For galloping through the halls. For sneaking into the pool when it was closed. For snapping towels in the locker room when someone could lose an eye or a testicle. For going off in the corner when the singing started, and whooping and giggling and cat-calling like a bunch of hoodlums from the South Side.

BARNEY. Do I have to say all that?

CHARLES. You should find your own words, of course.

BARNEY. Can I say balls instead of testicles?

CHARLES. Now watch it.

BARNEY. But I can't *do* it, Dad.

CHARLES. Well you've got to.

BARNEY. (*Setting his jaw, carefully.*) Well I won't. (*Pause. Charles turns to face him.*)

CHARLES. What did you say?

BARNEY. I said I won't. (*Another pause. Charles stares at him. Barney holds his ground defiantly.*)

CHARLES. Then you'll stay in here until you do. Merry Christmas! (*He strides out of the room, slamming the doors behind him.*)

BARNEY. (*Calling after him.*) I still won't! (*Then louder.*) I'll never apologize! (*Even louder.*) NEVER! (*Pause; then tentatively.*) Screw you, Dad! (*Pause. More confidently.*) Go frig a pig, Dad! Go fuck a duck! (*He gives the door the finger; he gives the door his whole arm. He grabs a long polo mallet and gives that to the door. Then he gives it to the stuffed heads, one by one. Then he tosses it away and looks around for an escape. He sees the door at L., goes to it, opens it, goes in, comes out in a moment.*) Cripes!

13

(*He slams the door, looks around, goes to the window, gets it open, climbs out on the sill, looks down, gets ready to jump as: The door to the hall opens, slowly, and Eleanor comes in. We hear singing behind her: "Bring the Torch, Jeanette, Isabella; Bring the Torch to the Stable Run." Eleanor looks about fourteen: she wears a dark velvet dress with a lace collar, long hair with a velvet ribbon in it, and black shoes. She comes in hesitantly as if looking for someone. Then suddenly she sees Barney poised on the window ledge. She screams.*)

ELEANOR. Don't JUMP! (*Her scream startles him so that he loses his balance and almost falls. But he grabs onto a mullion and saves himself. He sees her, remains on the windowsill, halfway in, halfway out.*)

BARNEY. Close the door! "

ELEANOR. What? (*It's hard for her to hear since he's half outside and the music is behind her.*)

BARNEY. Close the goddam door!

ELEANOR. Oh. (*She closes the door.*)

BARNEY. (*Standing on the sill.*) Otherwise, he'd try to prevent my escape.

ELEANOR. Who?

BARNEY. My father.

ELEANOR. Why?

BARNEY. He hates my guts.

ELEANOR. But why?

BARNEY. Because I'm not like him.

ELEANOR. Were you really going to jump?

BARNEY. Sure.

ELEANOR. Really?

BARNEY. (*Posing.*) Sometimes a man's got to risk his life for freedom.

ELEANOR. Gosh.

BARNEY. (*Standing at the railing.*) Who are you?

ELEANOR. Eleanor.

BARNEY. Eleanor who?

ELEANOR. (*Awkwardly holding out her hand.*) Eleanor Gilbert.

BARNEY. Never heard of you.

ELEANOR. (*Awkwardly letting her hand fall.*) We're visiting here.

BARNEY. Oh.

14

ELEANOR. We're guests of the Robbinses.
BARNEY. Never heard of them.
ELEANOR. Well I've never heard of you either.
BARNEY. That's because I haven't told you my name.
ELEANOR. Well what is it, then?
BARNEY. Barney Rusher.
ELEANOR. Never heard of you.
BARNEY. Well you better start, kid. My ancestors are plastered all over these walls.
ELEANOR. (*Indicating stuffed head.*) Is that one of them?
BARNEY. (*Laughing.*) Yeah, well, my father's president of this club. I can bowl here whenever I want, and play billiards even on weekends.
ELEANOR. Then why do you want to jump out the window? (*Pause.*)
BARNEY. Maybe I won't. (*He closes the window.*)
ELEANOR. (*Crossing to steps.*) Were you one of those noisy boys out there, during the singing?
BARNEY. Maybe.
ELEANOR. Yes you were. You were one of those rowdy boys off in the corner.
BARNEY. Maybe I was, maybe I wasn't.
ELEANOR. I was watching the whole thing. You were the ringleader.
BARNEY. All right. I was.
ELEANOR. You stood out like a sore thumb.
BARNEY. You were watching, huh?
ELEANOR. I watched your father throw you in here, too.
BARNEY. He didn't throw me in here.
ELEANOR. I saw him grab your arm.
BARNEY. I *walked* in here. He followed. (*Pause.*) Anyway he's not my real father. (*Pause.*) I'm an adopted child. (*He sits on railing.*)
ELEANOR. A what?
BARNEY. An adopted child. It's obvious. My mother had an affair with someone else. I'm not sure who, exactly, but I think it might have been Errol Flynn.
ELEANOR. Oh sure.
BARNEY. (*Jumping down from railing.*) Really. Oh my father forgave her. He probably got her to make a speech, and apologize.

15

ELEANOR. Oh sure. Any day.

BARNEY. It's *true*. And then they went on and had my brother Billy and my mother got so bored she died. (*He falls onto couch, D. R.*)

ELEANOR. I just don't believe that.

BARNEY. (*Sitting up.*) Do you believe I'm adopted?

ELEANOR. I—don't know.

BARNEY. (*Jumping onto table.*) I must be. I'm so different. But I know that somewhere else in this world I have a twin, who's adopted too. And someday we'll meet, and recognize each other, and—click. (*Pause.*)

ELEANOR. Would you do me a big favor?

BARNEY. Depends on what it is.

ELEANOR. Would you continue this conversation out there?

BARNEY. Why out there?

ELEANOR. Because I've got this mother. I'm supposed to meet people my own age, and I want her to see that I've done it.

BARNEY. Was that your mother standing by the piano?

ELEANOR. Yes.

BARNEY. That fussy lady?

ELEANOR. That was her—she—her. Do you want to meet her?

BARNEY. No thanks.

ELEANOR. Well you don't even have to. All you have to do is talk to me out there. If we run out of steam, you could introduce me to one of your friends.

BARNEY. (*Shaking his head.*) Uh-uh. Can't do it.

ELEANOR. Oh please. You don't know what it's like to be new some place. Everyone stares at you.

BARNEY. I like that.

ELEANOR. I just hate it. I could sink through the floor.

BARNEY. Maybe that's why I hack around all the time. So people will notice me.

ELEANOR. I noticed you, all right.

BARNEY. I saw you noticing. That made me do it all the more.

ELEANOR. I *thought* so. That's why I followed you in here. I thought you were the most exciting person there. (*Pause, they look at each other.*)

BARNEY. What was your name again? I might give you a call and take you to the movies.

ELEANOR. Eleanor Goldberg.

BARNEY. *Gold*berg?

ELEANOR. (*Quickly.*) I mean, Gilbert.

BARNEY. Which is it?

ELEANOR. Gilbert.

BARNEY. Why'd you say Goldberg?

ELEANOR. We changed it to Gilbert.

BARNEY. Are you Jewish?

ELEANOR. (*Quickly.*) No.

BARNEY. My father says anything ending with berg is Jewish.

ELEANOR. My father is Jewish. My mother made him change his name.

BARNEY. Where's your father?

ELEANOR. Back in Harrisburg.

BARNEY. Harrisburg's Jewish.

ELEANOR. Well my mother comes from here, and she's High Episcopalian.

BARNEY. What's so hot about that?

ELEANOR. Nothing. It doesn't make any difference what you *are*, anyway.

BARNEY. Come on. We'll go to the movies.

ELEANOR. (*Backing away,* L.) I don't like prejudiced people.

BARNEY. I'm not prejudiced. *They're* prejudiced out there. That's why we should go to the movies.

ELEANOR. What do you mean?

BARNEY. If they find out you're a Jew, they'll kick you right out.

ELEANOR. I don't believe you.

BARNEY. They will. They don't allow Jews in here. I've heard them say it. (*Mimicking them.*) If you let one Jew in, they bring all their friends, and pretty soon, they're all over the place. In the squash courts, in the pool, in the bar . . . and you can't say anything without getting into an argument.

ELEANOR. You're prejudiced!

BARNEY. No I'm not.

ELEANOR. You most certainly *are!*

BARNEY. See? Argument!

ELEANOR. (*Walking away.*) Oh honestly.

BARNEY. *(Grabbing the polo mallet.)* Come on. Let's go to the movies. It's *Robin Hood.* I'll lead you down the back way, and if anyone tries to persecute you, I'll run him through. *(He protects her with his "sword.")* Come on. Got any money?

ELEANOR. Won't you please come out there with me?

BARNEY. Can't. If I did, I'd just end up one of them.

ELEANOR. What's so bad about that?

BARNEY. It'd kill me, that's all. I'd die. (*He falls melodramatically on his sword. The door bursts open. Charles puts his head in angrily.*)

CHARLES. (*To Barney.*) I'll give you five more minutes! (*He sees Eleanor.*) Excuse me, young lady, but this boy has five more minutes! (*He turns, goes out, slamming the door.*)

ELEANOR. That was your father, wasn't it?

BARNEY. No. That was just someone I pay to tell me the time. (*Eleanor laughs in spite of herself.*)

ELEANOR. You *are* kind of funny.

BARNEY. I got that joke from a movie.

ELEANOR. What did he mean, five more minutes?

BARNEY. (*Climbing the book ladder.*) Oh well, he just meant that in five more minutes, he's going to drag me out into that public square, and tie me to the piano, and light a fire under me, and burn me alive for being a heretic. And before I can surrender my soul to heaven, while my flesh is crackling like a leg of lamb, he's going to reach into the flames and grope around in my chest cavity, and hold up to the hooting multitude my warm, red, palpitating, human heart! And so. . . . (*He reaches the top.*) To prevent that from happening. . . . (*He jumps to the railing.*) To rob him of that obscene pleasure. . . . (*He grabs an old bell-pull.*) I have no choice but to bid you farewell! (*He swings to windowsill, jumps off, disappears. Eleanor screams and runs up to the window. Before she gets there, Barney's head pops up casually.*) It's O.K. There's a roof here.

ELEANOR. (*Embarrassed for showing concern.*) You are a show-off, aren't you?

BARNEY. I sure am.

ELEANOR. Is that *all* you do? Just show off for people?

BARNEY. (*Looking at her.*) Oh no. I'm a very deep guy. Ug-glug-glug. (*He holds his nose and disappears as if he were going under water. She rushes to the window, stands half-waving, romantically, looking after him, then closes the window. The door opens. Singing*

18

*can be heard: "O Come, All Ye Faithful." Myra, Eleanor's mother,
stylishly dressed, fortyish, and fussy, comes in. She stands looking
at Eleanor for a long moment. Then she shakes her head and closes
the doors.)*

MYRA. Eleanor, dear love, what are you doing in this musty old room?

ELEANOR. I was just . . .

MYRA. .I've been combing the woods for you. Are we playing Hide-And-Seek at the age of fourteen?

ELEANOR. Oh no. *(Proudly.)* I was talking to a boy, Mother.

MYRA. *(Looking around.)* Boy? What boy? I don't see any boy.

ELEANOR. *(Indicating window.)* He just . . . he . . . *(She
looks at bell-cord, looks at window, looks at Myra, gives up with
a sigh.)* Oh golly.

MYRA. *(Patiently.)* The boys are out *there*, Eleanor. Boys and parties happen to occur around pianos and people.

ELEANOR. I get so shy, Mother.

MYRA. That's part of your charm. You just don't realize. How could you, sitting around Harrisburg, playing chess with your father? Now go have fun!

ELEANOR. I'll try. *(She starts glumly for the door.)*

MYRA. Chin up, shoulders back, smile. *(Eleanor stiffens her
shoulders, turns at the door with a ghastly fake smile.)* That's it.
The boys will gather like flies.

ELEANOR. What if they run away? *(Glances at window.)*

MYRA. Don't let them. Pretend you're having a perfectly marvellous time.

ELEANOR. *(Losing heart.)* I can't pretend . . .

MYRA. Of course you can. That's what growing up is. Pretend that party is for you.

ELEANOR. Oh not for me . . .

MYRA. As far as I'm concerned, that is your party. *(Leads her to
the couch.)* My sweet lamb, you have only five more years, at the
most, before everyone goes to college, and gets married, and scatters to the four winds. You've got to stake your claim, sweetie pie.

ELEANOR. Oh Mother . . .

MYRA. You do. This is the time and this is the place. In fact, I've decided to stay, dear.

ELEANOR. You mean, for supper?

MYRA. I mean . . . for supper. Now go find some *salle de bain* and comb your hair. And then you and I together will rejoin the human race. (*Eleanor gets up.*) Go on. Shoo. There's still the shank of the evening to go. (*Eleanor goes to the door, opens it, turns, squares her shoulders, gives the ghastly forced smile, and goes out. The music is heard softly from the hall: "Deck the Halls with Boughs of Holly." Myra watches Eleanor go, then turns to the audience, leaving the door open.*) Well I almost spilled the beans, didn't I? Couldn't help it. This place, this party. I was riding the crest of the wave. (*Comes* D.) Because I've finally decided to do it. I've decided to divorce Myron Gilbert. We have been at each other's throats since square one. This visit was a trial separation. I've tried. I'm separating. (*Glancing toward the party offstage.*) Eleanor will be fine. She can see her father any time she wants. But she won't want to. Not after she's lived here. Oh she'll be right in the swim of things before she knows it. She's lucky, actually. (*She takes a compact out of her purse, snaps it open, powders her nose, looks at herself in the compact mirror.*) When I was her age, my father changed his job, yanked us out of town, and dragged us around the country, not knowing a soul. Naturally I married the first man to look in my direction. What a life, wandering the face of the earth, chained to a stranger, frantically seeking out every second-rate bridge group and garden club and church supper, looking for some sense of connection. Never again! Not for me, not for her! We have come home. This is it. This club. This is the real thing. My mother told me about it, and it's true. Everything happens here; parties, dances, weddings. The whole life of this great city congeals right in this building. And that is why I paid sixty-three dollars for that velvet dress, and why I got Mimi Robbins to take us on, and why I want Eleanor out by that piano with everyone else. We'll stay here, and I'll launch her here, and she'll pick and choose and marry a man here, and she'll know what it means to be happy for the rest of her life! (*Charles comes in, looks around.*)

CHARLES. Oh excuse me. I was looking for my son.

MYRA. I'm afraid there's nobody here but us chickens.

CHARLES. I'm sorry. Have you lost your way?

MYRA. *Au contraire.* I've found it, after fifteen long years. (*She holds out her hand.*) Myra Gilbert. We're with the Robbins.

CHARLES. (*Taking her hand, bowing.*) Charles Rusher.

MYRA. I know. You're the man we should thank for this spectacular *soirée*.

CHARLES. You're most welcome.

MYRA. I believe your son is out there, playing the piano.

CHARLES. That's my younger son, Bill. I was looking for Barney, the older.

MYRA. Well I don't know about him, but I do know the piano-player is an absolute dream-boat. I have a daughter who's dying to meet him.

CHARLES. (*Offering her his arm.*) Then let's get them together.

MYRA. All right, let's. And maybe, after we've all struggled through a few more Christmas carols, we can talk people into some dancing!

CHARLES. Why not! (*They go out as the singing comes up loud: "O come ye, o come ye to Bethlehem." Then the music immediately modulates to a loud Lester Lanin-like dance tune from the early fifties, played by a party orchestra: something like " Green-Up Time." The lights from the hall spill into the trophy room. Through the window outside, we see the city lit at night. The branches in the foreground might have blossoms on them. Barney and Eleanor swirl into the room from the hall, dancing well together. Barney is in a black tuxedo, Eleanor in a long evening dress with white gloves. They do a couple of elegant spins to the music which wafts in, and then Barney, in a particularly deft turn, slyly kicks the doors closed as they spin by. The music becomes very faint, the only light is from the moon through the window.*)

ELEANOR. Hey!

BARNEY. (*Sexily, still dancing.*) Hmmm?

ELEANOR. (*Breaking away from him.*) Open that door.

BARNEY. What's the matter?

ELEANOR. I said open that door, please.

BARNEY. Aw, El.

ELEANOR. I want that door open, please. Right now, Barney. (*Barney looks at her, goes to the door, turns the key, locks the door, takes the key out, tosses it into the air, then puts it in his pocket.*) Very funny, Barney. Ha, ha. Big joke.

BARNEY. (*Imitating Brando.*) You and I have had this date from the beginning, Blanche.

ELEANOR. I want to *dance*, Barney.

BARNEY. O.K. (*He opens an old air vent or the transom over the*

21

door, the music wafts in, faintly.) See? (He bows to her.) Let's dance. (They dance briefly, more passionately, then she breaks away.)

ELEANOR. No, seriously, Barney. Really. I don't like this. I was out there dancing with Billy, and you just grabbed me.

BARNEY. That's called cutting in.

ELEANOR. That was not cutting in. Cutting in is reasonably polite. You just grabbed. (She goes to the door, tries it, turns.) Give me the key, please.

BARNEY. Nope.

ELEANOR. Barney, I want the key to this door, please.

BARNEY. Nope.

ELEANOR. (Turning on the lights, returning to him.) Well what do we do then? Stand here, eyeing each other?

BARNEY. I've got a bone to pick with you, El.

ELEANOR. About what?

BARNEY. I've got a gripe with you.

ELEANOR. About WHAT?

BARNEY. How come you're going to Bermuda tomorrow with Billy for the rest of the spring vacation? (Pause.)

ELEANOR. Who told you?

BARNEY. The word got out.

ELEANOR. Who told you?

BARNEY. (Angrily.) THE WORD GOT OUT, EL!

ELEANOR. You see? That's why is was a secret. Because you always yell bloody murder.

BARNEY. Damn right.

ELEANOR. Whoever told you was a big fat stinker.

BARNEY. You said it. It was your mother.

ELEANOR. Oh.

BARNEY. She told me I could just stop telephoning you after today.

ELEANOR. I'm going to Bermuda, Barney. A whole bunch of us are going.

BARNEY. She said you organized the whole goddam thing! You didn't even ask me.

ELEANOR. Because I knew you wouldn't go.

BARNEY. (Crossing D. R.) Damn right I wouldn't go. Frolicking around that crumby island with a bunch of superficial preppies!

ELEANOR. See? See the way you are? Well I want to go, and I'm

22

going. I've had to babysit on the Cape for two summers to pay for it, and I can't stand it around here during the slush season and I've seen all the movies with you, and I want to go to Bermuda.

BARNEY. Who's paying for Billy?

ELEANOR. I don't know and I don't care.

BARNEY. I know. My father's paying for him.

ELEANOR. Maybe he is.

BARNEY. He'd never pay for me.

ELEANOR. Well he's mad because you flunked out of college.

BARNEY. I didn't flunk. I left. Because they wouldn't let me on the fencing team.

ELEANOR. I don't blame them. You wanted to do it like Robin Hood.

BARNEY. Well Jesus. Who wants to just stand there?

ELEANOR. (*Sitting in chair.*) I don't know, Barney, but I want to go to Bermuda and have some fun.

BARNEY. You'll have fun, all right.

ELEANOR. I'm certainly going to try.

BARNEY. You'll get *laid* down there, El!

ELEANOR. Oh Barney.

BARNEY. You will! You'll get laid! I know that scene, El. All those blonde Ivy-League pricks running around in Madras shorts. They'll play volleyball with you, and then take you out on a motorbike, and get you all hotted up, and then you'll get *laid!*

ELEANOR. Barney, I promise . . .

BARNEY. You will! And then it'll be all over. (*He sinks onto the couch.*)

ELEANOR. Barney, trust me, for God's sake.

BARNEY. I don't trust *them*. They'll drag you into the poison ivy. They'll spill beer all over you. They'll get you all sandy. They'll barf! And then they'll go back to their grubby, sweaty, Greek-letter fraternities and stand around in the showers and scratch themselves and brag about you.

ELEANOR. I'll be with Billy.

BARNEY. (*Getting up.*) Then Billy will lay you, the sneaky little son-of-a-bitch! Oh gosh, El! Stay here with me.

ELEANOR. There's nothing to do here, Barney. The snow's gone. The skiing's over.

BARNEY. We could do it right, El.

ELEANOR. Do what?

23

BARNEY. It. *JJ*. We could make it, El. Right here. Right now. You and me. We could—bang. (*Pause.*)

ELEANOR. I could bang on that door, Barney, unless you give me that key.

BARNEY. No listen, El, really. Tonight's the night. And this is the place. You know we can't get into a hotel, and everyone says it's no fun in a car, and if we go to your place, your mother starts farting around, and if we go to mine, that son-of-a-bitch Billy hangs in there, so this is it, El, here, right here, where we first met. (*Eleanor looks at him, then runs to the door.*)

ELEANOR. (*Pounding.*) Help! (*Barney grabs her arm, brings her back to couch.*)

BARNEY. No, listen, El, *please*. Will you just *listen*? I've got it all figured out. Just give me two minutes, just *two*, and then if you don't like the idea, I'll open the door and take you back to Billy. O.K.? (*Pause.*)

ELEANOR. O.K. (*She sits down on the edge of the couch, suspiciously.*)

BARNEY. O.K. Now. Here's what we do. (*He looks at his watch.*) It's late. Billy will think you were tired, I took you home.

ELEANOR. Hey, just a—

BARNEY. (*Sitting at her feet.*) Will you *wait*? Meanwhile, I've already moved my car around the corner, and I've called your mother and told her it broke down so you're sleeping over at Lucy Dunbar's. O.K.?

ELEANOR. (*Standing up.*) *Not* O.K.!

BARNEY. (*Forcing her to sit.*) Will you let me *finish*? Now Lucy's parents are in Florida, so her grandmother's there, who doesn't know diddly-squat, and I've told my father I'm staying over at a friend's, so everyone thinks we're somewhere else! We're covered, El! All the way! All the way down the line! We can stay here tonight, and bang, right on this couch, we can bang all we want, we can bang two or three times if we feel like it, El. What do you say? What do you say, El? (*Long pause. She looks at him, then gets up and starts pounding on the door.*)

ELEANOR. Help! Somebody! Help!

BARNEY. (*Leaping over couch, grabbing her.*) Aw hell. (*He carries her D. R.*)

ELEANOR. (*Shrieking.*) Help! Rape!

BARNEY. (*Kneeling at her feet, arms around her waist.*) Jesus, El. We're not kids anymore. You'll be in college next year, and I'll be

24

drafted and sent to Korea to *die!* Oh this is it, El! I know it! If I don't get you tonight, I'll lose you forever! (*Eleanor looks down at him affectionately. Knocks are heard on the other side of the door.*) VOICES. Anybody in there? (*The handle is turned, the door rattled.*) Anybody there? (*Eleanor continues to look at Barney.*) It's locked. Guess no one's there. Maybe it was someone downstairs. (*Voices fade away.*)

ELEANOR. (*Quietly.*) Barney, sweetie, I love you dearly, but Bermuda is all planned.

BARNEY. (*Bouncing up.*) So's this. This is planned. Look. (*He hurriedly drags a large suitcase out from the couch by the fireplace.*) Look what I smuggled in this afternoon!

ELEANOR. What's that?

BARNEY. Just wait. (*With a sweep, he clears the large oaken table* D. L. *of its sporting magazines.*) I'm going to make Bermuda look silly.

ELEANOR. (*Skeptical.*) Oh Barney.

BARNEY. (*Opening the suitcase.*) Just give me a CHANCE, El! At least let me get into the game! (*He spreads an elaborate tablecloth on the table, quoting:*)

"Then by the bed-side, where the faded moon
Made a dim silver twilight, soft he set
A table, and, half-anguished, threw thereon
A cloth of woven crimson, gold, and jet . . ."

(*To Eleanor.*) That's from "The Eve of Saint Agnes." Did you read that in school?

ELEANOR. Yes.

BARNEY. (*Setting out silver candlesticks.*) I doubt it. It's a little raunchy for Miss Muff's in the Mountains or wherever it is you go. We had to memorize it. It's about this great love affair in the Middle Ages.

ELEANOR. I know what it's about.

BARNEY. Then you'll know that . . . (*He continues to set the table with silver dishes quoting:*)

"He, from forth a suitcase brought a heap . . .
Of candied apple, quince, and plum, and gourd
With jellies soother than the creamy curd . . ."

ELEANOR. (*Taking up the poem.*)

". . . . And lucent syrups, tinct with cinnamon;
Manna and dates, in argosy transferred . . ."

BARNEY. (*Looking at her.*) Hey!

ELEANOR. We had to learn it, too . . ."From Fez"—
BARNEY. (*Joining her.*)
   "From Fez, and spiced dainties, every one,
   From silken Samarcand to cedared Lebanon."
(*He has finished setting the table with goodies. From the air vent, music wafts in: a romantic song from the early 50's.*)
ELEANOR. Did you steal all that?
BARNEY. No.
ELEANOR. (*Eating a cookie.*) Mmmm. Toll House cookies. And the chocolate's still soft inside.
BARNEY. Made 'em myself. And there's banana ice cream, unless it's melted.
ELEANOR. Oh it's my favorite!
BARNEY. I know. And smoked oysters, which are supposed to be terrific for sex. (*He produces the oysters and ice cream side by side.*)
ELEANOR. Barney— (*She crosses* D. L.)
BARNEY. The only thing I stole was this. (*Brings out a bottle of wine.*) From my father. (*Reads the label.*) Chateauneuf du Pape. (*Looks at her.*) Unless you prefer Mogen David.
ELEANOR. Just cut that out.
BARNEY. (*Going to table, taking the silver cup.*) We'll drink it from this. The Holy Grail. The city-wide mixed doubles invitational tennis cup. Which my mother and father won in 1933. (*He kneels in front of her again.*)
ELEANOR. The only reason I'm going along with this, Barney, is to see what you'll do next.
BARNEY. (*Handing her matches and a corkscrew.*) Here. Light the candles. Open the wine. (*He looks at her, then turns.*) I've got to go pee. (*He goes into the bathroom.*)
ELEANOR. (*Calling after him.*) You're absolutely crazy, Barney! You know that, of course. (*She eats another cookie.*) Mmmm. These cookies are divine. I'll have a bite with you, Barney, because I can see you've worked hard over this. But that's that. (*She lights the candles.*) And if someone comes in, I'm going to sink through the floor.
BARNEY. (*From the bathroom.*) No one can come in. There's only one key.
ELEANOR. And I'm going to Bermuda, Barney. I'll have one glass of wine with you, for old time's sake, but if you try anything else,

I'm going to scream my head off. (*Barney comes out of the bathroom wearing an exotic bathrobe.*)

BARNEY. Hi.

ELEANOR. Oh my God.

BARNEY. It's my father's. What do you think?

ELEANOR. Oh Lord. What next?

BARNEY. This. (*From behind his back, he produces a black lacy negligée.*) Like it? I got it on sale.

ELEANOR. Help.

BARNEY. Put it on and we'll have a midnight supper.

ELEANOR. I'll stay as I am, thank you.

BARNEY. (*Hanging it by the fireplace.*) Suit yourself. I'll put it here for when you change your mind.

ELEANOR. I'll never change my mind, Barney. (*He goes back into the bathroom.*)

BARNEY. (*From within.*) Sure you will.

ELEANOR. Never.

BARNEY. Wait till you see this. (*He comes back out with a huge protuberance in the front of his bathrobe.*) Stick 'em up.

ELEANOR. (*Shrieking.*) Oh HEAVENS!

BARNEY. That's just a preview of coming attractions! (*He pulls a toilet brush out from under his bathrobe, tosses it back into the bathroom.*)

ELEANOR. (*Bursting into laughter.*) Oh Barney, you absolute imbecile! (*She collapses onto the couch in laughter. He rushes to join her, sits down beside her, begins to kiss her. The music through the vent changes to "Goodnight, Sweetheart." Eleanor, sitting up.*) The party's ending.

BARNEY. I know . . .

ELEANOR. Oh Barney, let's go out there.

BARNEY. (*Indicating his bathrobe.*) Like this?

ELEANOR. Let me go out there then.

BARNEY. (*Indicating the spread table.*) What about that?

ELEANOR. I don't know what to do.

BARNEY. When in doubt, dance. (*He pulls her up from the couch, they dance to the music very slowly, very affectionately.*) I love this push music.

ELEANOR. Barney, just shut up, please. Just shut your trap for once, O.K.? (*They rock together. Suddenly Barney shudders and freezes.*)

27

BARNEY. Uh-oh.

ELEANOR. What?

BARNEY. Never mind.

ELEANOR. What's the trouble?

BARNEY. I said never MIND.

ELEANOR. Well I mean—

BARNEY. I just had a little accident.

ELEANOR. You what?

BARNEY. (*Turning away.*) I had a little ACCIDENT! (*Pause.*)

ELEANOR. (*Getting it.*) Oh. (*She carefully extricates herself. Pause.*) Well. That does it, doesn't it.

BARNEY. Not at all. I'll be right back. (*He goes into the bathroom, slams the door. The music ends. Through the vent, we hear the sounds of conversation. The party is breaking up.*)

ELEANOR. (*Calling off to Barney.*) The party's over, Barney. Everyone's leaving. I want to leave too. I don't want to stay here tonight, sweetie. Really. I don't. (*She picks up a cookie, takes a bite, shakes her head, puts it down.*) I want my eight hours sleep. I want to go to Bermuda, Barney. I want to lie around in the sun with Billy and the whole gang. I want to play tennis and hear the Whiffenpoofs at the Elbow Beach Club. What's wrong with that, Barney? What's wrong with people having fun? I love all that, Barney. I love all those people. They're good-looking, and they play games, and they know all the lyrics to all the songs. (*Pause.*) You don't, Barney. You can't sing and your tennis is terrible. You're bad for me, Barney. Mother says so, and it's true. Every time I get with you, I get all mixed up. That's why I arranged Bermuda. You're too much for me, Barney. (*She blows out the candles.*) I don't love you, Barney. I love Billy. He was editor of the Year Book, and he's going to Princeton in the fall, and he wants to be a lawyer. You? You couldn't even stay in Franklin and Marshall. What kind of a future would I have with you? I want a home. I want a family. I've never had them. I'll never get them with you, Barney. Barney? Did you hear me, Barney? (*Silence. Then the sound of a shot from within the bathroom. Barney staggers out, stark naked except for a bloody towel clutched to his gut. He falls face down onto the couch by the fireplace. Eleanor screams, then sees the gun dangling from his hand. It is obviously a cap gun. Eleanor takes his hand, lets it fall.*) Oh Barney! It's that same fake gun you used last summer. And probably the same ketchup. Jesus,

28

Barney. Now you're even repeating yourself. Grow up! (*There is banging on the door.*)
VOICES. (*From outside.*) What happened? Who's in there? Open the door.
ELEANOR. (*Whispering.*) Barney, get up! Please!
VOICES. Who's hurt? Somebody hurt in there? (*Eleanor frantically starts to clear the table, dumping the stuff back into the suitcase.*)
ELEANOR. Barney, help! For God's sake!
BARNEY. (*Lifting his head.*) Only if you don't go to Bermuda.
ELEANOR. (*Defiantly.*) Never! (*Barney falls melodramatically back onto the couch.*)
MYRA'S VOICE. (*From outside.*) Eleanor! It's your mother! Are you in there, dear?
ELEANOR. (*Frantically clearing.*) Barney, I'll never forgive you for this. Never!
CHARLES'S VOICE. (*From outside.*) Barney? I'm coming in there, Barney. (*To others outside.*) Wait. I think I've got a master key.
ELEANOR. (*Closing the suitcase, shoving it behind the couch.*) This is it, Barney. This is the END! (*A key is heard rattling in the door. Eleanor tosses the tablecloth to Barney, who covers himself. She turns bravely to face the door. The door bursts open. Myra and Charles come in, both in overcoats over their night clothes, they take one look and turn back to the hall.*)
CHARLES. (*As if to crowd in hallway.*) It's all right, everybody. Go home. I'll handle this. (*Eleanor has noticed the black nightie, still hanging by the fireplace. She quickly grabs it, shoves it under her dress. Charles and Myra close the doors behind them, enter the room.*)
MYRA. (*Indicating the prone Barney, the defiant Eleanor.*) You see? You see why I telephoned you! Car breaking down, my eye!
CHARLES. (*Infinitely patient.*) What's the story, Barney?
MYRA. I might ask you the same question, Eleanor. With the door locked.
CHARLES. Barney, I am waiting for an answer.
BARNEY. (*Carefully.*) I got drunk. Took a shower. Passed out. She found me here and locked the door so I wouldn't be embarrassed.
CHARLES. (*Skeptically.*) They heard a shot. A scream.

29

BARNEY. I was goofing around with that old starter gun. (*To Eleanor.*) Sorry, El. (*Pause.*)

MYRA. Eleanor, Billy is out there, and I'm sure he'd be delighted to take you home. (*Eleanor looks at her, looks at Barney, and then walks slowly and stiffly out, the black nightie dragging behind her.*)

CHARLES. Barney, get up, and go into that bathroom, and put your clothes on. You're coming home with me. (*Barney gets up, wrapping the tablecloth around him. Myra turns discreetly away. Barney goes into the bathroom and closes the door. Myra draws her overcoat around her ample bosom.*)

MYRA. I don't think we heard the whole story, Charles. There was obviously some hanky-panky going on. But I think it's safe to say we nipped it in the bud.

CHARLES. You were right to telephone, Myra.

MYRA. I hope I didn't wake you up.

CHARLES. (*Covering up his pajamas.*) Not at all. I was reading in bed.

MYRA. Oh. So was I.

CHARLES. Really? What book?

MYRA. You'll laugh.

CHARLES. Not at all. Tell me.

MYRA. *The Black Rose.* By Thomas B. Costain. Am I hopelessly middle-brow?

CHARLES. No, no.

MYRA. Actually, it's quite risqué.

CHARLES. Is it?

MYRA. Yes. It tries to give an accurate picture of what went on in the Middle Ages.

CHARLES. What did?

MYRA. (*Looks at him, laughs flirtatiously.*) Won't tell.

CHARLES. (*Carefully.*) Well I imagine whatever went on then . . . still does.

MYRA. Oh yes. Oh yes. Absolutely. (*Pause. He notices her bosom.*)

CHARLES. (*Quickly calling off.*) Hurry up there, Barney.

MYRA. Of course, now, with all this confusion, I doubt if even a good book will do it.

CHARLES. Do it?

MYRA. Put me to sleep.

CHARLES. You might try an aspirin.

MYRA. Does that do it?

CHARLES. Sometimes. (*Pause. He glances again at her bosom. Then calls off.*) We're waiting, Barney.

MYRA. I must confess, sometimes I resort to a nightcap.

CHARLES. So do I.

MYRA. I always feel very sheepish, dipping into the Scotch, all by myself.

CHARLES. I know the feeling.

MYRA. Perhaps you'd like to stop by and join me? (*Pause.*)

CHARLES. But we'll have Barney.

MYRA. (*With a sigh.*) Oh. Yes.

CHARLES. And Eleanor will be there. With Bill.

MYRA. Yes. (*Pause.*) Of course, I intend to send her right to bed. She has to get up at the crack of dawn for Bermuda.

CHARLES. Yes. Bill should go to bed, too.

MYRA. Eleanor will go out like a light, of course. She sleeps like a top. (*Pause. Her overcoat has unaccountably fallen open again, to reveal some some magnificent cleavage.*)

CHARLES. I see. (*Suddenly calling off.*) Barney, we can't wait any longer! You'll have to get home by yourself. And don't wait up! I am having a nightcap with Mrs. Gilbert! (*He takes Myra's arm and quickly escorts her off, taking a good sidelong look at her bosom. They leave the door to the trophy room open. As they leave. crowd sounds and music come up from off R.; a piano, accordion and bass playing a bouncy version of "For Me and My Gal." The lights come up on the trophy room. It is a bright late afternoon in early summer. The curtains are open and through the windows we see blossoms on the branches. Eleanor comes in from the hall. She wears a white bridal gown in the style of the mid-fifties, carrying her train over one arm.*)

ELEANOR. (*Softly; furtively.*) Barney? Are you in here, Barney? (*She looks behind the couch.*) Barney, where are you? (*She knocks on the bathroom door.*) Barney? (*She opens the bathroom door, looks in. Then she climbs to the balcony, goes to the window, opens that, looks out.*) Barney? (*She leaves the window open, sighs; speaks to herself.*) Well I've done it, anyway, Barney. I've married Billy, and we're going to be happy, and there's nothing you can do about it now. (*Charles comes in, now dressed in a cutaway. The sounds of the wedding party come up loud behind him.*)

CHARLES. When do I get a chance to dance with the bride?

31

ELEANOR. (Brightly.) Oh any time. Any time at all.

CHARLES. What brings you in here, of all places?

ELEANOR. I—I thought I might find Barney.

CHARLES. Barney?

ELEANOR. I thought he might be hiding.

CHARLES. Eleanor, sweetheart, he's in San Francisco.

ELEANOR. But he might just *arrive.*

CHARLES. How can he? The Navy wouldn't let him. His ship sails today for the Far East.

ELEANOR. I know, I know.

CHARLES. That's why we set this date!

ELEANOR. I just have this awful feeling . . . (*Charles looks at her, then closes the door behind him, shutting out the music.*)

CHARLES. Let me show you something. (*He crosses to the cup,* D. L.) You see this cup? My wife and I won this in 1933. Our names are right here.

ELEANOR. I know.

CHARLES. You've seen it?

ELEANOR. Someone showed it to me once.

CHARLES. It's been here forever. Look. Here's the dent from 1912 when old Mrs. Stevens grabbed it from the winning couple and threw it at her husband.

ELEANOR. Why did she do that?

CHARLES. She hated to lose. Everyone wanted to win in those days. My wife Helen and I tried every year after we were married. And never came close. Until 1933. When we won hands down.

ELEANOR. What made you win?

CHARLES. We found our rhythm. There wasn't a point we played that we weren't in tune. It was absolutely exhilarating.

ELEANOR. It sounds ideal.

CHARLES. It was. It was so ideal that I've never married again. I don't think I could ever find that rhythm with anyone else.

ELEANOR. Oh that's sad.

CHARLES. No, because we had a good thing going. And good things go. But I can remember it. And reflect on it. And recognize it in others. I see it in you and Bill.

ELEANOR. Our game has its problems.

CHARLES. That's what I'm saying. You have to practice, you have to play. And some day you and Bill will have your names on this cup.

ELEANOR. I hope so. (*Charles puts the cup back.*) Do you think Barney will ever be on it?

CHARLES. I used to hope so.

ELEANOR. But not any more?

CHARLES. He doesn't have any staying power. He gets all wound up, but it doesn't last.

ELEANOR. (*Reminiscently.*) I know . . .

CHARLES. He leaves himself wide open. That's why Bill always beats him.

ELEANOR. Maybe he doesn't want to win.

CHARLES. Not at mixed doubles, anyway. But you wait. He'll come back from the Navy and turn into a champion—what? Bowler. He loves knocking things down. Now come on. Let me trot you around that dance floor.

ELEANOR. All right. (*The door bursts open. Myra comes in, all gussied up in a flowered dress, with hat and gloves.*)

MYRA. Here you are. Eleanor, poor Billy is out there surrounded by old ladies.

ELEANOR. Oh, poor guy! (*She rushes out. Myra watches her go, then closes the door and turns to Charles.*)

MYRA. Oh Charles, guess what just arrived.

CHARLES. What?

MYRA. A wedding present. Special delivery to the club.

CHARLES. From Barney?

MYRA. From your elder son.

CHARLES. I'm delighted he finally sent one.

MYRA. You won't say that when you hear what it was. I took the liberty of opening it.

CHARLES. Go on. (*Myra sits at the desk, D. R. Charles follows.*)

MYRA. It was a picture frame.

CHARLES. What's wrong with that?

MYRA. A silver picture frame. From Gump's.

CHARLES. What's wrong with Gump's?

MYRA. Nothing's wrong with Gump's. Gump's is one of the finest stores in San Francisco. It's what was *in* the frame that's wrong.

CHARLES. Well what was, Myra?

MYRA. His picture.

CHARLES. Barney's picture?

MYRA. Barney's picture was in that frame.

33

CHARLES. Well I think that's rather touching. I should have a picture of Barney in his sailor suit. I'll put it on the piano.

MYRA. He wasn't in his sailor suit.

CHARLES. Oh?

MYRA. He was in his birthday suit.

CHARLES. (*Exploding.*) Barney sent, as a wedding present, a picture of himself in the NUDE?

MYRA. Full front. Eleven by thirteen. In kodacolor.

CHARLES. Oh good Lord! (*He sits on couch, D. R. Myra follows him.*)

MYRA. And . . .

CHARLES. *And?*

MYRA. How do I say this?

CHARLES. How do you say WHAT?

MYRA. He had this great big white bow tied around his—dingy. (*She sits beside him on the couch.*)

CHARLES. (*Striking his head.*) Oh, oh, oh.

MYRA. And . . .

CHARLES. (*Anguished.*) AND? AND?

MYRA. There was a note.

CHARLES. SAYING WHAT?

MYRA. Saying "wish we could be there."

CHARLES. Oh God, oh God, oh God.

MYRA. Thank heavens he's a million miles away, Charles.

CHARLES. That's what I told Eleanor.

MYRA. Absolutely. And that's what I told those two sailors downstairs.

CHARLES. (*Looking at her.*) Sailors?

MYRA. Yes. Sailors. I think they were sailors. Except they wore leggings and armbands and carried nightsticks, like policemen.

CHARLES. (*Jumping up, grabbing her.*) Shore Patrol! What the hell did they want?

MYRA. They wanted Barney. So I said he was on his ship for the Far East. They asked if they could wait outside. I said there was no point, but they could. And I sent them each down a glass of champagne. Because they're defending us all against communism.

CHARLES. I'd better talk to them.

MYRA. All right Charles. (*Indicates bathroom.*) I'm going to powder my nose. The downstairs ladies room has been occupée all afternoon with tipsy bridesmaids. I'll see you on the dance floor.

(*Charles hurries out as Myra crosses to the bathroom. After a moment Barney appears at the window in a white sailor suit. He climbs in stealthily, looks around. The party sounds waft in; the music might be playing "The Girl That I Marry." He watches the party for amoment. From the bathroom comes the sound of flushing. He starts, turns, hides. Myra begins to sing again, from within: "Ding, dong, the bells are gonna chime!" Barney gets an idea: he grabs an old gun from the gun racks on the wall. He hides behind the couch, R. The bathroom door opens, and Myra backs out, priming as if at a mirror, clucking, singing, "Get me to the church on time." She stops, adjusts her girdle, stops again, straightens a seam, stops again to brush off some lint. When she is at C.:*)

BARNEY. (*Suddenly popping out with the gun.*) O.K., baby, reach!

MYRA. (*Jumps, gasps.*) Barney!

BARNEY. (*Waving the gun.*) One peep out of you, I'll plug you from your guzzle to your snatch!

MYRA. Oh Barney, no . . . (*Barney threatens her with the gun.*)

BARNEY. Now. Go to the door, open it, and call your daughter in here.

MYRA. (*Pleading.*) Barney . . .

BARNEY. DO IT! (*She jumps. They sidle together to the door.*) Open it slowly. (*She does.*) Not too far. (*She has it open a crack. The sounds of the party come up: "Her nails will be polished and in her hair/She'll wear a gardenia, and I'll be there." Barney stands behind her so he can't be seen.*) Can you see her?

MYRA. (*Weakly.*) She's dancing with Billy.

BARNEY. Call her.

MYRA. (*Weakly waving.*) Yoo-hoo. (*Turning to him.*) There's too much going on.

BARNEY. Get somebody to get her.

MYRA. (*Hastily, as if to someone in the hall.*) Oh Roger? Roger Bliss, would you ask Eleanor to come in here. I . . . I . . . (*She looks hopelessly over her shoulder at Barney.*)

BARNEY. You're drunk. You're sick. You've got the whirlies!

MYRA. (*To hallway.*) I'm—having trouble with my slip . . . thank you, Roger.

BARNEY. Good. (*He closes door.*)

MYRA. (*Desperately backing toward C.*) Oh Barney, please, please, PLEASE leave her alone! Let her be happy, Barney, please!

BARNEY. She'll be happy with me.

35

MYRA. She's married, Barney. They've got furniture. They've got *lamps!*

BARNEY. She can return that crap.

MYRA. But she doesn't *want* to, Barney.

BARNEY. She can return Billy.

MYRA. She *loves* Billy.

BARNEY. Wrong! She loves *me!* (*The door opens. Eleanor comes in, sees Barney, quickly closes the door behind her.*)

ELEANOR. Goddam it, Barney. I knew it.

MYRA. He's got a gun, Eleanor. (*Barney goes through an elaborate gun drill.*)

ELEANOR. (*Walking up to Barney.*) Give it to me, Barney. (*He hands it to her.*) He's always playing with fake guns, Mother. (*Tosses the gun onto the couch.*)

BARNEY. (*To Eleanor.*) I have to see you.

ELEANOR. Let me talk to him, Mother.

MYRA. Eleanor, I'm not going to—

ELEANOR. I can handle it, Mother.

MYRA. Eleanor, I won't allow—

ELEANOR. (*Forcefully.*) Get *out* of here, Mother!

MYRA. (*Backing out.*) Yes. All right. Yes. (*She opens the door.*)

ELEANOR. And close the door after you, please. Tell Billy I'm fixing my dress. Period.

MYRA. Yes. Oh yes. Oh dear. (*Myra goes out, closing the door behind her. Eleanor faces Barney.*)

BARNEY. (*Saluting her.*) Hi.

ELEANOR. Oh Barney. How'd you get here?

BARNEY. I went AWOL and grabbed a plane . . . let's go. (*Indicating window.*) I've got a Hertz-U-Drive-It hidden in back.

ELEANOR. Barney, I'm married to Bill!

BARNEY. Fair enough. He gets the wedding. I get the honeymoon. . . . Come *on!*

ELEANOR. (*Backing away.*) You're on some ship.

BARNEY. Hell, that's halfway to Hawaii.

ELEANOR. Then you're a deserter!

BARNEY. No, no. I'm a conscientious objector. I object to Billy. You do the same!

ELEANOR. Oh I don't know where I am!

BARNEY. It doesn't matter, as long as you're not here. Come on. Out the window. We'll drive all night. We'll change clothes,

36

change cars, change lives. We'll cross borders, El. Name your border, and we'll cross it. Skiing in Canada, swimming in Mexico, which do you want?

ELEANOR. It's like some movie . . .

BARNEY. (*Moving toward her.*) What's wrong with that? Here's what they do in the movies.

ELEANOR. (*Backing toward steps to balcony.*) Stay away from me.

BARNEY. I just want to kiss the bride.

ELEANOR. You just stay away.

BARNEY. Movies are better than ever. (*He corners her on the stairs. They kiss. She responds. The door bursts open. Charles rushes in, followed by Myra, who shrieks.*)

CHARLES. (*To Myra.*) Close the door. Quickly. (*Myra does; Charles surveys Barney.*) Young Lochinvar out of the west, eh? About to sweep the bride off her feet, Barney?

BARNEY. We were just leaving, Dad.

CHARLES. Oh no you're not.

BARNEY. We are, aren't we, El?

ELEANOR. (*Anguished, going to window.*) I don't know!

MYRA. Eleanor!

CHARLES. Nobody's leaving except you, Barney. And you are leaving quietly, down the backstairs, where the Shore Patrol is waiting to fly you back west.

ELEANOR. (*Turning from window.*) Shore Patrol?

MYRA. Two of the nicest boys. One's even a Negro.

CHARLES. Will you go, boy, or will you cause trouble?

BARNEY. I'm going out the window, and she's coming with me. Now stand back. (*He leaps to the windowsill, holding Eleanor behind him, as if she were Maid Marion.*)

ELEANOR. (*To Barney, breaking away.*) How'd the Shore Patrol know?

CHARLES. (*Going to door.*) All right, Barney. I'll bring them up here, and we'll have a very messy scene.

MYRA. Oh Charles, how ghastly!

ELEANOR. Wait! Please wait. (*Charles stops. She turns to Barney.*) How'd they know you were here, Barney?

BARNEY. I don't know.

ELEANOR. What made them come here? Right to this club? Right in time for the reception?

BARNEY. I don't know.

ELEANOR. Did you tell someone you were coming here?

BARNEY. No. I—

ELEANOR. You told people, didn't you?

BARNEY. I just told—

ELEANOR. You told *every*one! You told your buddies, you told your captain . . .

BARNEY. I didn't tell the captain!

ELEANOR. You probably sent a wire to President Eisenhower, saying "Help, bring in the cavalry at the last minute!"

BARNEY. I might have told—

ELEANOR. Oh Barney, you left a trail a mile wide!

BARNEY. (*Looking at her, scratching his head.*) Maybe I did.

ELEANOR. You were just playing games, weren't you? You didn't even want to win.

BARNEY. Maybe I didn't.

ELEANOR. (*To Charles and Myra.*) He never wanted to. Ever.

BARNEY. Oh, El . . .

ELEANOR. (*Squaring her shoulders.*) O.K., Barney. You can keep on playing. You can play Robin Hood right now. You can have your Merry Men rush in here, and ruin my wedding. You can do that, Barney. Or you can grow up, and get the hell out of here, quietly, down the back way. Which is it, Barney? (*Pause.*)

BARNEY. I'll go quietly.

MYRA. Then there is a God.

CHARLES. They said you could meet your ship in Hawaii, Barney. (*Barney goes to Charles, holds out his hand.*)

BARNEY. Goodbye Dad. (*They shake hands.*)

CHARLES. And I'll call someone in Washington. We'll get you off with a light punishment. (*Barney goes to Myra, holds out his hand.*)

BARNEY. Goodbye, Mrs. Gilbert.

MYRA. (*Coldly, refusing to shake hands.*) Frankly, Barney, I think it will do you a lot of good if they put you in the clink or the jug or the mess or whatever it is they put you in. (*Barney shrugs, crosses to Eleanor, who is still on the balcony by the window.*)

BARNEY. Goodbye, El. (*Eleanor holds out her hand for him to shake.*)

ELEANOR. Goodbye, Barney. (*He takes her hand, then suddenly kisses it passionately.*)

BARNEY. I still love you, El. (*Eleanor quickly withdraws her hand.*)

CHARLES. (*Threateningly.*) Get going, Barney! (*Myra opens the door. Out he goes.*)

MYRA. Eleanor, I think you and Bill should be changing for your wedding trip. (*Eleanor nods and starts for the door.*)

CHARLES. And don't look so sad, Eleanor. The next time you see Barney, he'll be just another member of the family.

MYRA. Exactly. This sort of thing will never, never happen again.

ELEANOR. (*Turning in the doorway.*) Oh I know. That's what's so sad. (*She goes off.*)

MYRA. (*Crossing* D. C.) How can she say a thing like that?

CHARLES. Because she'll miss him. So will I.

MYRA. He pointed a GUN at me, Charles!

CHARLES. Oh, Myra, he's harmless. Look, it's just one of those old things off the wall. Here. I'll put it back. (*He picks it up. It goes off with a bang, knocking down one of the stuffed heads. Myra screams, stands aghast. Charles looks at the gun, looks at Myra, looks at the door. The lights fade quickly.*)

END OF ACT ONE

ACT TWO

The early sixties. Afternoon. The greenery outside the window indicates mid-summer. The window is open, the door is open. Through the door, we hear sounds of a baby crying and other children's voices, and the murmurs and laughter of a small gathering. Someone on the piano might be playing musical comedy selections. After a moment, Barney and Eleanor come in together from the hall, arm in arm. Eleanor wears a summer dress and carries a knitting bag, and Barney wears conventionally collegiate summer clothes: seersucker jacket, khakis, shirt and tie. He carries a gin and tonic.

ELEANOR. *(As they enter, indicating the room.)* See? Nothing's changed.
BARNEY. *(Remaining at door.)* Except us.
ELEANOR. Mmmm. Well come on *in.* We haven't had a chance to catch up.
BARNEY. *(Indicating door.)* Shall I . . . ?
ELEANOR. Um. No. Better leave it open. Just in case.
BARNEY. In case what?
ELEANOR. In case the baby needs me. *(She sits on the couch* D. L.)
BARNEY. Oh.
ELEANOR. You look marvelous. That California sun.
BARNEY. You look fine, too.
ELEANOR. Me? Oh I'm a cow. Since the baby. Since three babies. I'm two sizes larger. Upstairs.
BARNEY. Lucky baby.
ELEANOR. Now, now.
BARNEY. Lucky Billy.
ELEANOR. I said, now, now. *(Pause; she pats the couch. He sits beside her.)* Barney, I want you to know how much I appreciate your coming all the way for the christening.
BARNEY. I wanted to. For my own god-son, after all.

40

ELEANOR. But from San Francisco!

BARNEY. Oh I hitched a ride. With friends. It was O.K.

ELEANOR. Where'd you go after the church? We all got worried.

BARNEY. I just came right here.

ELEANOR. Here?

BARNEY. I was hot. I took a quick swim.

ELEANOR. You still like it here, then?

BARNEY. Can't stay away. (*Pause.*)

ELEANOR. Thank you for the christening present, by the way.

BARNEY. That's all right.

ELEANOR. A silver spoon. It was lovely.

BARNEY. Well, you know. Born with it in his mouth. Might as well face up to these things.

ELEANOR. Mmm. Frankly, when I was opening it, I was a little nervous.

BARNEY. Really?

ELEANOR. Yes. I thought you might come up with something ghastly which would shock the pants off everybody.

BARNEY. Were you disappointed?

ELEANOR. (*Too insistently.*) No. Of course not. No. (*Pause.*) But I wanted you to be his godfather, Barney. I stuck to my guns on that.

BARNEY. Why?

ELEANOR. Oh . . . I don't know. My third child. Probably my last. I thought *some*body in my family should have some connection with something outside these . . . walls.

BARNEY. That's why I came.

ELEANOR. What do you mean?

BARNEY. I needed some connection *in*side. (*Pause. They look at each other. From through the door, the sound of a baby crying.*) Don't you want to . . . ?

ELEANOR. He just needs changing. Billy will do it. He's terribly helpful. (*The piano stops. The crying subsides.*) See? (*Pause. Eleanor takes out her knitting.*) Now I want to hear all about you. It's been so long, Barney.

BARNEY. I took a second hitch in the Navy, I finished college on the G.I. Bill . . .

ELEANOR. Oh I know *that*, Barney. I want to hear the gory details. In the Navy, for example. Did you sew your wild oats?

BARNEY. I tried.

41

ELEANOR. I'll bet you did. Did you have any romantic adventures?

BARNEY. Sure.

ELEANOR. Can you talk about them?

BARNEY. Sure. Do you want to hear what happened one June, in Rangoon, during a monsoon, with a baboon?

ELEANOR. No thank you . . . so you won't talk about your adventures.

BARNEY. I'll talk about one.

ELEANOR. Go ahead.

BARNEY. I got married.

ELEANOR. (*Shocked.*) Barney!

BARNEY. Oh not legally. But married. She was Japanese.

ELEANOR. (*Flippantly.*) Oh gosh. *Madame Butterfly. Sayonara.* All that.

BARNEY. It was serious, El. I lived with her whenever we were in port. We had a little house. Made a little nest. I even mowed a little lawn.

ELEANOR. Just like me and Bill.

BARNEY. (*Looking at her.*) Right.

ELEANOR. Well what *happened?*

BARNEY. I wanted to bring her home. I went to the embassy, filled out the papers, everything . . . and then suddenly, I chickened out.

ELEANOR. Because of the club?

BARNEY. Because of you. (*Pause.*)

ELEANOR. Oh.

BARNEY. I was still playing *games!* That was just a Japaneses imitation of you and Bill. I was still competing with my brother, halfway around the world!

ELEANOR. Poor girl.

BARNEY. Poor *me.* I'll never love anyone, El.

ELEANOR. Oh phooey.

BARNEY. Never. I know that now. I'm doomed to live alone.

ELEANOR. You'll find someone.

BARNEY. Nope. It wouldn't be fair. I'd always be comparing her to you. (*Pause.*)

ELEANOR. Barney, tell you what: now you're back, why not stay? Bill and I have this marvellous house out in Fairview. We've fixed it all up. You could come out to dinner. Once a week, even. A regular thing. I'm a marvellous cook, Barney. We'll have these marvellous meals. And there's a guest room. You could spend the night. Any time. You'd be a breath of spring, out there, actually. Bill works his tail off, and I don't seem to get beyond the washer and the dryer, and the kids see nothing but green grass. You'll open us up, Barney. You'll be like one of those fabulous uncles in children's books - - - Uncle Wiggly, Doctor Doolittle. You'll take us where the wild things are. (*She sits on the edge of his chair, ruffles his hair.*)

BARNEY. Um, no thanks, El. (*He gets up, moves* D. L.)

ELEANOR. Why not? We need you out there.

BARNEY. No. I'm going back to Berkeley.

ELEANOR. That's silly. You've finished school.

BARNEY. No. I've just started. I'm going to get my Ph.D.

ELEANOR. On what, for God's sake?

BARNEY. I want to work on the Middle Ages!

ELEANOR. The Middle *Ages*?

BARNEY. That's my area. I know it cold. (*He moves to the raised area by the window.*) The Middle Ages are very much like this.

ELEANOR. (*Following him up.*) This?

BARNEY. A quiet, dull life, punctuated by ceremony . . .

ELEANOR. Oh . . .

BARNEY. A closed universe, halfway between the last Roman Emperor . . . (*Indicates a portrait on the wall.*) . . . and a new way of life . . . (*He looks out the window.*)

ELEANOR. I see.

BARNEY. I know that world. I'm half in, half out. I can study it, write about it, teach it.

ELEANOR. Will you teach "The Eve of Saint Agnes"?

BARNEY. Hell no. That was just an adolescent version.

ELEANOR. (*Leaning against a pillar.*) I suppose . . . well. That's fine, Barney. Very sensible. Very mature.

BARNEY. (*Looking at her, carefully.*) I'm going to focus in on the idea of courtly love.

ELEANOR. Courtly love?

BARNEY. There was a whole movement. Of guys who were in love with married women. Courtiers, jesters, fools . . .

ELEANOR. And what did they do?

BARNEY. They wrote these fantastic love poems. They worshipped from afar.

ELEANOR. Is that all they did? Just—write poems?

BARNEY. They wrote, they went on quests—they sublimated.

ELEANOR. Didn't they ever just—come around?

BARNEY. Not much.

ELEANOR. Why not?

BARNEY. It was too dangerous. (*Long pause.*)

ELEANOR. Well. I think we should be joining the others, don't you?

BARNEY. (*Getting up.*) Yes I do. (*Charles comes in hurriedly, closing the door behind him. He looks older, is dressed in a summer suit.*)

CHARLES. I'm sorry to interrupt, but I've just had to call the police.

ELEANOR. The police?

CHARLES. There's trouble. Old Mr. Sidway went down to take his afternoon dip, and what did he find but three naked Negroes and a woman, all splashing around in the pool! They've obviously broken in, and the police will have to get them out.

BARNEY. They're my guests, Dad.

CHARLES. They're your WHAT?

BARNEY. I rode with them from Berkeley. They were hot. (*Charles stands looking at him, dumbfounded.*)

ELEANOR. (*Quietly, exultantly.*) Welcome home, Barney. (*Pause. Charles looks from one to the other, then speaks with great restraint.*)

CHARLES. Eleanor, I wonder if you'd tell the police we were mistaken.

ELEANOR. Yes. All right. (*She goes out quickly.*)

CHARLES. And Barney, I want you to go down to the pool, and ask your friends to put on their clothes, and come up to the main room, and raise a glass to my new grandson. Go on, Barney. Do it. (*Barney looks at him, then goes out. The lights begin to dim on the trophy room. Charles continues to, speak, as if to himself.*) I will greet them, I will shake their hands, I will see that they are made comfortable, because they're guests, and the cardinal rule of this club is hospitality. And if I hear one rude remark from anyone in the room about these—guests, then whoever makes it will feel my full fury. And then, when the party's over, when these guests have decided to depart, I am going to do something which I should have done ten years ago. (*Turning to audience.*) I am hereby

44

blackballing my elder son! He is no longer welcome here, now or in the future. I will speak to Alice in the coatroom, and Fred in the bar, and John in the locker room, and if they see hide or hair of him, ever again, they should call me, or the police, or the National Guard! I want him OUT! Permanently and forever! (*He paces.*) We have always prided ourselves on our openness here. I like to think we are a democratic institution. In recent years, we have admitted many fine Jewish members, and there's talk that Walter Fay is partly Chinese. Fine. Good. But we are not ready for the invasion of naked barbarians. Poor old Mr. Sidway was profoundly disturbed by what he saw. He seems to have had a slight stroke. Fortunately, Doctor Russell was here. I told him to send Barney the bill. (*He sighs.*) Now I wish him well in Berkeley. I hope he works hard. I even hope he comes home, now and then, to visit. He's my son, after all, and I love him. But when he returns, he may not—repeat not—come to this club. If he wants to swim or play a game, let him seek out some public facility. If he wants to have a drink with old friends, let them meet in some gloomy saloon. If he wants to cash a check, let him stand in line at the bank. Oh we'll still break bread together, he and I. We'll still do that. But not here. Oh no. We will go out. To a restaurant. We will be shown to a dirty table in a dark corner by a cheap woman who chews gum. After an endless wait, she will bring us two watery cocktails, crackers wrapped in cellophane, call us "honey," and serve us luke-warm coffee with the main course. That's what democracy is these days. That's what Barney wants apparently. And I'm sorry. (*He crosses the stage to read a magazine, getting older by the step. The lights come up as Myra comes on in a pantsuit, also looking older. Her costume suggests the late sixties.*)

MYRA. (*Hesitantly.*) Charlie . . . (*He turns to her.*) There was a telephone message at the desk. I told them I'd give it to you.

CHARLES. Yes?

MYRA. Long distance. From California. From you-know-who.

CHARLES. Go on.

MYRA. He needs money again.

CHARLES. Why?

MYRA. For bail. Again.

CHARLES. What did he do this time?

MYRA. What difference does it make? It's all the same. Marching without a permit, lying down in front of troop trains, picketing against poor Mr. Nixon.

CHARLES. How much does he need?

MYRA. It's higher this time.

CHARLES. How much?

MYRA. A thousand. (*Pause.*)

CHARLES. What time do the banks close these days?

MYRA. Oh Charlie, you're not going to keep *doing* this.

CHARLES. He hasn't got a dime.

MYRA. Whose fault is that? He lost a perfectly good teaching job. Because he *stole*, Charles.

CHARLES. He didn't *steal*, Myra.

MYRA. He stole private *property*, Charles.

CHARLES. It was public property.

MYRA. He stole the university president's *car*. And drove it *around*.

CHARLES. He didn't keep it. He gave it to the poor.

MYRA. He gave it to Angela *Davis*.

CHARLES. Well Angela Davis is poor, Myra. Quite poor. I don't believe Angela Davis has a net worth of more than—

MYRA. Charlie, *honestly*!

CHARLES. (*With a sigh.*) Oh Myra, I'm suddenly very tired.

MYRA. So am I, Charlie. So am I. Tired of seeing you tear yourself apart over that boy. Charlie, he is simply *de trop*. Now you've got a wonderful, hard-working son and a lovely daughter-in-law, and three marvelous grandchildren—

CHARLES. They tire me too.

MYRA. Charlie!

CHARLES. They do. I don't like it out there. Those noisy meals, the television blaring away, the endless chatter about schools. I don't like it out there much.

MYRA. Why Charlie: you're getting old.

CHARLES. That's it. Old. And I want to be with people my own age. (*He looks at her.*) Let's get married, Myra.

MYRA. Charlie!

CHARLES. Why not?

MYRA. I thought you were tired.

CHARLES. I am. Let's lean on each other in our autumn years.

MYRA. But Charlie . . .

CHARLES. Think about it. Take your time. I'll go see about that

46

boy. (*He goes off. Myra looks after him, looks at audience, ponders very briefly, clears her throat.*)

MYRA. After long and careful thought, I have decided to marry Mr. Charles Rusher, of this city. It will be a small, sober ceremony, family only, I probably won't even wear a hat. Then a few friends back here afterward for a quiet drink. A glass of champagne, maybe, French champagne, and I hope someone will get on his feet and make a toast. There might be music. I could bring in that accordian player from the Park Plaza who plays nothing but Fred Astaire. Which means someone might want to dance . . . (*She begins to sing, dance.*) "Heaven . . . I'm in Heaven . . ." (*Stops.*) And let there be food. Chicken in patties and peas. Oh hell, let's have a party! Let's have a biggie! Let's have the most spectacular get-together since the Cerebral Palsy Ball! (*Charles appears at the door.*)

CHARLES. Myra . . .

MYRA. (*Swirling to him.*) Oh Charlie, yes, yes, YES!

CHARLES. (*Patting her hand.*) That's fine, dear. You make the arrangements. I've got to rush to the bank before they close. (*He goes out. She stands looking after him, then comes slowly* D.)

MYRA. Make the arrangements, make the arrangements, Myra . . . Strange . . . my first husband used to say the same thing. Wouldn't drive, wouldn't carve, wouldn't . . . never mind what he wouldn't do. Oh why do I seem to attract such exhausted men? Or are they only exhausted when they get to me? (*She sits down.*) Why can't I be exhausted once in a while? What if I said No. I refuse. I am hereby *hors de combat.* (*She leans back, closes her eyes.*) Oh this is marvellous. (*She opens her eyes, sits up.*) But then who will move him out of that great barn of a house and into a nice apartment? And who will remind him to take his pills? And who will get him to think about his will, and the college education of three grandchildren? (*She stands up, squares her shoulders.*) Me! I'll do it! Myra Rusher will make the arrangements! I'll plan the trips and manage the meals and send out the Christmas cards year after year! And when things fall apart, I'll hold them together with Scotch Tape and Elmer's Glue and Gilbey's Gin! Somebody has to do these things! On my head be it! *Apres moi, le deluge!* I'll arrange things until the day I die! Then I'll arrange my own funeral! Nobody else will bother, that's for sure! (*The lights come up on the trophy room. She defiantly takes a tape*

47

measure out of her pocket and begins to measure a chair, getting older with each move. Through the open doors we now hear the sounds of women's voices. After a moment, Eleanor comes in, in a trim shirt and pants, suggesting the early seventies. Through the window, the red and brown shrubbery now suggests early autumn, late afternoon.)

ELEANOR. (Stands for a moment, watching Myra.) Mother. What are you doing?

MYRA. I am measuring this ratty old furniture. I plan to put slip-covers on everything I can get my hands on.

ELEANOR. Why?

MYRA. Because no one else will.

ELEANOR. Not this room, Mother. Please. Leave it just the way it is.

MYRA. (Huffily.) All right. You're the boss, after all. This is your day.

ELEANOR. Oh not just mine, Mother. (She goes to the window, looks out.)

MYRA. Well I mean, you fought for it. You won. It's primarily because of you that women now have the run of the club every Thursday.

ELEANOR. (At the window, vaguely.) We all fought.

MYRA. Well you were the leader. (Looks at her.) Why aren't you out there, enjoying it?

ELEANOR. I got a little bored, Mother.

MYRA. Well go bowl or play bridge or something! Go meet the new members. You can't just walk out on the whole shebang! I mean, if Charlie knew you were hiding in here after you fought tooth and nail for women to be out there, my God, he'd have another heart attack.

ELEANOR. (Suddenly.) He didn't even call me, Mother.

MYRA. Who?

ELEANOR. Barney.

MYRA. Oh Eleanor.

ELEANOR. I sat by the telephone all morning. He didn't even call.

MYRA. He was at the hospital, seeing his father.

ELEANOR. He still could have called.

MYRA. Eleanor, he's a busy man now. Or says he is. At least he seems to come and go every other minute.

ELEANOR. But he always calls.

MYRA. Well I can't stand here and sympathize with someone who doesn't receive a telephone call from a crazy brother-in-law. I've been sitting around hospitals for weeks. I'm going to try my hand at paddle tennis. (*She goes to the door, then turns.*) One thing sure. He can't come here! (*Myra goes out. Eleanor sighs, and turns back to look out the window. After a moment, a tall blonde woman backs into the room, wearing a raincoat and slacks. She closes the door stealthily behind her. Eleanor turns at the sound, faces her back.*)

ELEANOR. Yes? May I help you? (*The woman doesn't turn around.*) I don't believe we've met. Are you a new member? (*The woman turns to face Eleanor. A long moment. It's Barney, of course, in a wig.*)

BARNEY. No. I'm a guest. (*He tosses off the wig.*)

ELEANOR. (*With a shriek of joy.*) Barney!

BARNEY. Dad said it was woman's day, but faint heart ne'er won fair lady. (*He tosses off his raincoat, revealing a mod, mid-seventies outfit.*) So I bought a disguise. (*He puts the wig on a post of the balcony.*)

ELEANOR. Well it worked.

BARNEY. Oh boy, did it! One of the waiters tried to make a pass at me.

ELEANOR. (*Looks at wig.*) Wow. That must be a fifty-dollar wig.

BARNEY. That's O.K. I'm rich now.

ELEANOR. Doing what, Barney? Nobody can figure out what you do.

BARNEY. Oh I sell things, buy things.

ELEANOR. In San Francisco?

BARNEY. There, and New York. I've got apartments in both places.

ELEANOR. But what's your product?

BARNEY. Let's say I'm a middle man. As usual. As always. (*Looks at watch.*) And I'm in between planes. So fill me in on yourself.

ELEANOR. Oh. Me.

BARNEY. You. Dad says you're the high priestess around here now.

ELEANOR. Oh, I do my bit. I also have a part-time job. (*She comes down from the balcony.*)

BARNEY. Hey! Doing what?

ELEANOR. I'm a family counselor. I went back to school, like everyone else. Now I'm an expert in keeping families together on Mondays, Wednesdays, and Fridays.

BARNEY. Are you any good?

ELEANOR. Oh I'm terrific. We all get together in this hot, white room. And then we gripe, like mad. (*Pause.*) I gripe, too. (*Pause, she turns to him, hugs him.*) Oh Barney, it's so good to see you. If you hadn't come, I would have telephoned you, wherever you were.

BARNEY. Why?

ELEANOR. I got a vacation coming up. And I want to visit you.

BARNEY. Good God! With the whole gang?

ELEANOR. No, just me.

BARNEY. What about—Bill?

ELEANOR. Separate vacations are good occasionally, Barney. I've learned that much. He went duck-hunting with the boys last fall. The year before I visited my father. Now it's my turn again.

BARNEY. What about the kids?

ELEANOR. Oh. (*She laughs.*) They're big, Barney. They're huge. Bill can spoon out their spaghetti. Or they can do it themselves. No, I want *out* for a couple of weeks, Barney. I want to visit you.

BARNEY. Where?

ELEANOR. New York. I love New York. I'll come the next time you're there.

BARNEY. That might be a little tricky, El.

ELEANOR. Why? You could take me in tow. You probably have all these weird, wonderful New Yorky friends.

BARNEY. (*Mock-sophisticated.*) Oh I do, I do.

ELEANOR. Then— (*Looks at him.*) Ah-hah. (*Pause.*) You've got a girl there.

BARNEY. Right. (*He sits on the arm of the couch.*)

ELEANOR. She lives in your apartment.

BARNEY. Right.

ELEANOR. Do you love her?

BARNEY. No.

ELEANOR. But you *like* her.

BARNEY. When I'm there.

ELEANOR. And I might mess that up.

BARNEY. You might mess *me* up. (*Pause.*)

ELEANOR. Then I'll come to San Francisco.

BARNEY. El . . .

ELEANOR. You've got a girl there too.

BARNEY. Yes.

ELEANOR. Do you love *her*?

BARNEY. God, no . . . she's married.

ELEANOR. Then let me *visit* you. Send her back to her husband.

BARNEY. No.

ELEANOR. Why the hell not?

BARNEY. I'm also involved with the husband. (*Pause.*)

ELEANOR. What?

BARNEY. I like the husband, too. (*Pause.*)

ELEANOR. Oh God.

BARNEY. You asked.

ELEANOR. Oh Jesus, Barney. (*She turns away, comes* D. *Pause; then turns back to him, brightly.*) Who do you like the best?

BARNEY. I don't know. I like them all.

ELEANOR. I can't *stand* this. Do they know about each other?

BARNEY. Sure.

ELEANOR. They do?

BARNEY. Sure.

ELEANOR. Aren't they jealous of each other?

BARNEY. Not at all.

ELEANOR. Have they all *met* each other?

BARNEY. Sure.

ELEANOR. They *have*?

BARNEY. They've made it with each other.

ELEANOR. Oh no.

BARNEY. We've all made it together.

ELEANOR. Barney!

BARNEY. I told you I was a middle man.

ELEANOR. Yes. You told me.

BARNEY. And you might as well know what I do for a living.

ELEANOR. (*Walking* D. L.) I don't want to hear.

BARNEY. (*Following her.*) I'm in the film business.

ELEANOR. Oh well, at least that's half decent. (*Pause.*)

BARNEY. Decent's not quite the word.

ELEANOR. You make *pornographic* movies.

BARNEY. I don't like that word, either.

ELEANOR. What are they then?

BARNEY. They are films about physical love.

ELEANOR. Are you *in* these things?

BARNEY. Hell no. I'm not good enough. (*Quickly.*) I mean, I'm good, but not that good . . . you should go to one.

ELEANOR. No thank you.

BARNEY. Billy goes.

ELEANOR. He does not.

BARNEY. He does. He told me. And Jackie Onassis goes. And the Unitarian Church shows them on retreats.

ELEANOR. Well I won't go. (*She moves away from him, he pursues her.*)

BARNEY. There's one you ought to see.

ELEANOR. I doubt it.

BARNEY. You ought to. It was my idea. We based it on *Robin Hood.* It's called *The Arrow and the Quiver.*

ELEANOR. Christ, Barney.

BARNEY. It's good. It's very artistic. We won a special prize at Cannes.

ELEANOR. (*Suddenly reeling on him.*) I think it's disgusting.

BARNEY. Oh yeah?

ELEANOR. I think your whole life sounds cheap and sad and disgusting.

BARNEY. Oh yeah? And what about you? What do you do now, in the swinging suburbs? Don't you all throw your car keys in the center of the rumpus room, and go home with whoever picks them up?

ELEANOR. No.

BARNEY. I'll bet.

ELEANOR. You think I'd do that?

BARNEY. How do I know? I've kind of lost touch with the middle class. Maybe you've got something different going with those dykes out in the main room. (*Eleanor looks at him, hauls off and slaps him, hard. He looks at her, then slaps her back.*) Equality of the sexes, friend. (*He strides u. toward the door.*)

ELEANOR. Bastard! (*She hurls herself at him, begins to pummel him. He grabs her arms. They struggle. He holds her, then gives her a hard, passionate kiss. She struggles, then responds. Finally she breaks away, and goes to chair d. l. Barney leans against the balcony railing, panting.*)

BARNEY. The thing is . . . you don't realize this, but . . . by showing these films, we liberate people. There's a big connection between sex and politics . . . Open things up, spell things out, people will learn to be free . . . Hell, it's still Robin Hood, El . . . I'm still fighting the good fight.

ELEANOR. Do you really believe that? (*Pause.*)

BARNEY. No.

ELEANOR. I didn't think so.

BARNEY. (*Indicating window.*) Out there, I believe it. (*Looks at her.*) In here, with you, it seems like a pile of crap.

ELEANOR. Glad to hear it.

BARNEY. Forget your vacation, El. Stick around here. It's a decent place. (*Pause.*)

ELEANOR. Too decent for me, I'm afraid.

BARNEY. (*Coming down to her.*) That'll be the day.

ELEANOR. No, I mean it. Last summer, I almost had an affair.

BARNEY. Hey. Truth telling time. Who with? (*He sits on the arm of her chair.*)

ELEANOR. You don't know him. Neither do I, really. He stopped by one time before supper, collecting for the Heart Fund. Bill wasn't home yet, the kids were hanging around some game, I was slapping a meal together before I went to a meeting. So in he came. I offered him a sherry. We got along. We decided to meet in town for lunch, and all that. So I got down my Sierra Club calendar and he got out his Mutual of Omaha appointment book, and we tried to arrange a day, but we never could get our schedules together. Finally I gave him a check. For twenty-five dollars. For the Heart Fund. And he left.

BARNEY. Just as well.

ELEANOR. I guess. But the family's not enough any more, Barney. At least, not for me. I thought I could make this club into a place where different people could get together.

BARNEY. Well it worked, didn't it? Ladies Day, Open Membership, all that?

ELEANOR. Oh I don't know. I wanted to turn it into a kind of camp, every summer, when people were away. You know: ghetto kids playing games, learning to swim. I mean it just *sits* here. But they voted me down.

BARNEY. What did you expect?

ELEANOR. I guess half the fun of clubs is keeping people out.

BARNEY. Mmm.

ELEANOR. Well. I got what I asked for, anyway, Barney. I got in.

BARNEY. And I got out. And now where are we?

ELEANOR. Nowhere.

BARNEY. (*Arm around him.*) I'll always count on you, El. You keep me honest.

ELEANOR. Yes. Between New York and San Francisco.

BARNEY. You're different, and you know it. I happen to love you.

ELEANOR. Whatever that means.

BARNEY. It means a lot, these days. (*Pause. He looks at her, looks at his watch.*) Oh my gosh. My plane leaves in forty-five minutes. (*Looks at her again.*) Want to come along?

ELEANOR. With you?

BARNEY. Sure. (*Long pause.*)

ELEANOR. No. (*Pause.*)

BARNEY. Thank God. I couldn't deal with you out there.

ELEANOR. Well I can't deal with you in here, Barney. (*Pause.*) So maybe you'd better go.

BARNEY. Uh . . . huh. (*He gets up.*) It's goodbye, then. (*He puts on his raincoat.*)

ELEANOR. (*Not looking at him.*) Yes it really is.

BARNEY. (*Brightly.*) I mean, so long.

ELEANOR. I mean goodbye. (*Pause.*)

BARNEY. Christ. . . . (*No response. He gets the wig and puts it on.*) Hey. I better wear this. Maybe I can still get it on with that waiter. (*No response. He goes to the door, turns.*) Someday something will happen, El. Right here in this room, where we first met. And you'll know it, and I'll know it, and it'll be absolutely fantastic. (*He opens the doors and minces out exaggeratedly as we hear the women's voices come up. Eleanor gets up, goes to balcony, looks out window as Myra bustles in.*)

MYRA. (*Looking back down the hall.*) What a large woman that was. Do you suppose she's interested in bowling?

ELEANOR. She's from out of town.

MYRA. Oh. Well. Billy's on the phone, and he wants to know when he's supposed to put the pizza in the oven.

ELEANOR. Tell him I'll . . . (*Pause.*) Tell him . . . (*She starts to cry.*) Oh Mother, I don't want to go home.

MYRA. (*Rushing to hold her.*) Eleanor! Dear love! (*Eleanor sobs in her arms as the lights dim on the room. The lights come up on Barney, who is wheeling Charles into the room in a wheelchair. Charles looks old and weak, and is covered with a lap robe. Barney now wears a dark blue blazer.*)

54

CHARLES. (*As he is being wheeled* D. C.) Put me over there. Away from the draught . . . (*Looking around.*) I have the feeling I'm in this room for the last time.

BARNEY. Oh no, Dad. You're just having a bad day.

CHARLES. I'm all right. (*Pause.*) What brings you to town this time?

BARNEY. I just wanted to see you, Dad.

CHARLES. You need money?

BARNEY. No, Dad.

CHARLES. You won't get any more money from me.

BARNEY. I don't want money, Dad.

CHARLES. (*Indicating couch.*) Sit there.

BARNEY. (*Sitting on edge of chair.*) That's all right, Dad.

CHARLES. I said sit there.

BARNEY. (*Quickly.*) All right. (*He sits on the edge of the couch.*)

CHARLES. Will you see Eleanor this time?

BARNEY. No.

CHARLES. You sure?

BARNEY. I'm sure.

CHARLES. Thou shalt not covet thy brother's wife!

BARNEY. Neighbor's.

CHARLES. What?

BARNEY. It's "thy *neigh*bor's wife."

CHARLES. Doesn't matter. Nobody reads the Bible these days. (*Pause.*) They're separated now. You must know that. She's living in some miserable apartment. Can't make up her mind. Bursts into tears at parties. The children come and go. Billy sees another woman. It's very bad.

BARNEY. I'm sorry, Dad.

CHARLES. You damn well ought to be. You've been badgering the poor girl for thirty years!

BARNEY. Not any more, Dad.

CHARLES. She chose Bill.

BARNEY. I know, Dad.

CHARLES. You lost, Barney! You lost the game! Now get off the damn court! Do it! Promise me you'll leave her alone. We're not fooling around now. Promise. (*Pause.*)

BARNEY. I promise I'll stay away, Dad.

CHARLES. Thank you.

BARNEY. Unless she comes to me.

55

CHARLES. Fair enough. (*Pause.*) I hear you've got a lot of money.

BARNEY. A little.

CHARLES. A lot. Myra told me how you made it. Peddling smut. (*Shakes his head.*) I can't discuss it.

BARNEY. I've sold out, Dad. I'm through.

CHARLES. What does it matter, anyway? There are only a few more apples in the barrel for me.

BARNEY. Oh no, Dad.

CHARLES. Oh yes. I'm going, it's all going. The club is going, did you know that?

BARNEY. I heard.

CHARLES. Oh yes. It's on the market. Nobody wants to keep it up any more. The waiters steal, the pool leaks. The men don't have time to stop by after work. The women don't bother with lunch. So it's up for sale. They plan to build some bubble in the suburbs. Held up by thin air.

BARNEY. It won't be the same, Dad.

CHARLES. I don't know who will buy this damn thing. Even the Catholics can't afford it any more. Probably some developer will break it up into doctors' offices. People will be getting rectal examinations right here in this room. (*Pause, looks at him.*) Not that you care. You never liked the club anyway.

BARNEY. I did, Dad. I always came back.

CHARLES. Just to cause trouble.

BARNEY. Not always.

CHARLES. Always.

BARNEY. Not this time, Dad. I want— (*Pause.*) I want your blessing, Dad. (*Pause.*)

CHARLES. Do you know the story of the prodigal son? No, of course you don't. Nobody reads the—

BARNEY. I know it, Dad.

CHARLES. A man has two sons, one good, one bad. The bad son comes home, the father kills the fatted calf for him, even after all the trouble he's caused.

BARNEY. I remember, Dad.

CHARLES. That father was a fool.

BARNEY. (*With a sigh.*) Yes, Dad.

CHARLES. Bill gets the fatted calf. (*Pause.*)

BARNEY. Fair enough.

CHARLES. Well, he needs it, he has three children, he's stayed at the wheel all these years.

BARNEY. O.K. Fine, Dad. I'm with you.

CHARLES. And all you've ever done is break up the party. Am I right? Am I right, Barney? (*Pause. Myra appears at the door, in an older-looking dress.*)

MYRA. Barney, your taxi's here.

BARNEY. Thanks. (*Myra goes off. Barney gets up.*) I'd better go. (*He gives his father a quick kiss on his head and starts for the door.*) Goodbye, Dad.

CHARLES. Barney! (*Barney stops.*) Barney, there's a psychiatrist at the club, Jewish fella, I've forgotten his name, who told me once that the trouble with the world is that everyone wants to kill his father. Do you agree with that?

BARNEY. No.

CHARLES. And he said, if I understood him correctly, that's what you've been trying to do all your life. Trying to kill me.

BARNEY. (*With a groan.*) Oh no, Dad!

CHARLES. Because if that's true, you've succeeded.

BARNEY. Oh Dad, PLEASE! (*He kneels by the wheelchair.*)

CHARLES. (*Looking at him tenderly.*) Did you really come to town just to see me?

BARNEY. To see you, Dad, I swear.

CHARLES. Oh Barney, why have you been so difficult all these years?

BARNEY. Maybe I wanted *you* to see *me*. (*Charles stares at him for a long moment, touches him tenderly, then closes his eyes.*)

CHARLES. I'm very tired.

BARNEY. (*Getting up.*) Goodbye, Dad. (*Bends over, kisses him again and starts out.*)

CHARLES. Goodbye, Barney . . . thank you for stopping by. (*Barney goes off as Myra comes in.*)

MYRA. Goodbye, Barney. (*To Charles.*) Now I think it's time for our nap. (*She begins to wheel him out.*) And then we'll have our blue pills, and one cocktail, and two poached eggs with Walter Cronkite.

CHARLES. I want to change my will, Myra.

MYRA. Oh Charles, not again.

CHARLES. I want to make things fair and square.

MYRA. We'll discuss it later, Charles.

CHARLES. He's a good boy.

MYRA. Billy's a good boy.

CHARLES. They're both good boys. We didn't do so badly after all, Helen.

MYRA. Helen? Charlie, I'm Myra. Really I must ask you to stop confusing me with your first wife. (*She wheels him out as the lights darken. When they come up again, Barney is standing at the fireplace, holding his speech, dressed in his gray suit, as he was at the beginning. Eleanor comes in, in black again. A funeral prelude is heard.*)

ELEANOR. Now we really *are* ready to begin, Barney. (*No answer.*) I spoke to Mother, and she said yes, all right, read your speech. But please be brief. And respectful. (*No answer.*) Did you hear me, Barney?

BARNEY. (*Turning, passionately.*) I can't do it, El. I'd stand up there and cry like a goddam baby.

ELEANOR. (*Moving toward him.*) Oh Barney . . .

BARNEY. (*Tossing the speech onto the fireplace couch.*) You do it.

ELEANOR. Me?

BARNEY. (*Moving away from her.*) Go on. I'm staying in here. (*He goes to u. c. Eleanor picks up envelope, opens it, looks at speech.*)

ELEANOR. This isn't a speech, Barney. This is some . . . document.

BARNEY. (*His back to her.*) It's a deed.

ELEANOR. It's a what?

BARNEY. (*Coming d.*) It's a deed, it's a DEED. I went and bought the place.

ELEANOR. Bought it?

BARNEY. Bought the whole frigging CLUB! With the proceeds of my pornography business.

ELEANOR. But what for?

BARNEY. I don't know. I don't even know. I wanted to give it to the old man. (*He comes d. r.*)

ELEANOR. (*Following him.*) I think that's wonderful.

BARNEY. It was dumb. (*He tries to get away from her.*)

ELEANOR. I think it's fabulous.

BARNEY. It was just dumb. I'm a dumb clown. All my life making faces in front of the mirror. Still doing it, and the mirror isn't even here any more!

ELEANOR. I think it's the most fantastic thing. Oh Barney, I want to go out there and tell them.

BARNEY. Fine. Do that. And tell them to clear their smellies out of the locker room so I can have the place torn down. (*He crosses to chair* L. C., *sinks into it.*)

ELEANOR. Tear it *down*? You wouldn't do that!

BARNEY. What else can I do with the damn thing?

ELEANOR. I don't know . . . (*Reaching for it.*) What would Robin Hood do?

BARNEY. Oh El, come off it.

ELEANOR. No really. What does he do, at the end of the movie?

BARNEY. I don't remember.

ELEANOR. I remember. He wins this great contest and gets his castle back.

BARNEY. That does not happen.

ELEANOR. It does. I know it does.

BARNEY. What does he do when he gets it? Sit around? And pay huge property taxes to the Sheriff of Nottingham?

ELEANOR. Um. No. What he does is . . . lower the drawbridge. And open the gates. Everyone rushes in. There's singing and dancing all over the place.

BARNEY. Oh sure.

ELEANOR. It's true! And you have the feeling he'll turn it into a wonderful place. (*Pause.*) And Maid Marion helps him.

BARNEY. Take a look at the latest version. Robin dies in battle. Maid Marion is a nun.

ELEANOR. That's not my version. In mine, they get together and start the Renaissance. (*Myra comes in, in black.*)

MYRA. (*Looking from one to the other.*) Just what do you two think you're doing?

BARNEY. Dreaming.

ELEANOR. No. Planning.

MYRA. There happens to be a funeral going on. Eleanor, come with me. Billy's waiting.

ELEANOR. I'll come with Barney, Mother.

MYRA. Eleanor . . .

ELEANOR. And sit with him, too. In front of everyone. That's that.

MYRA. (*Taking a deep breath.*) This has been a long and difficult

59

day. I have lost a husband. Now apparently I am losing a daughter. What can I say? *Tant pis.*

BARNEY. Watch your language. (*Myra turns and starts out huffily. Barney calls to her.*) Hey. (*Myra stops, looks at him stonily. He gets up, goes to her, touches her hand.*) I'm sorry.

MYRA. Thank you, Barney. (*She goes out. Barney goes to the balcony, looks out the window.*)

ELEANOR. (*Carefully.*) I'll tell you something else Maid Marion does. When the service is over, she rides out to the supermarket, where she gets a box of Toll House cookies, a quart of banana ice cream, and some smoked oysters. Then she stops at the liquor store for some Chateauneuf du Pape. Then she returns to the castle, and opens the bottle, and pours it into this cup. (*She gets the cup from* D. L., *places it on the table* C.) Then she just waits to see who walks through that door. (*Pause.*)

BARNEY. Do you think . . . after all these years . . . I could walk through that door?

ELEANOR. (*Eyes closed, anguished.*) Couldn't you?

BARNEY. Hell no! I'd come through the window! (*He opens the windows wide and then comes* D. *to join her. Eleanor puts the deed in the cup, faces him. The funeral music begins offstage. People begin to sing: "A Mighty Fortress is Our God." Barney bows to Eleanor, offers her his arm. She takes it. They stride off joyfully, as if to their own wedding. The cup on the table catches the last of the light.*)

THE END

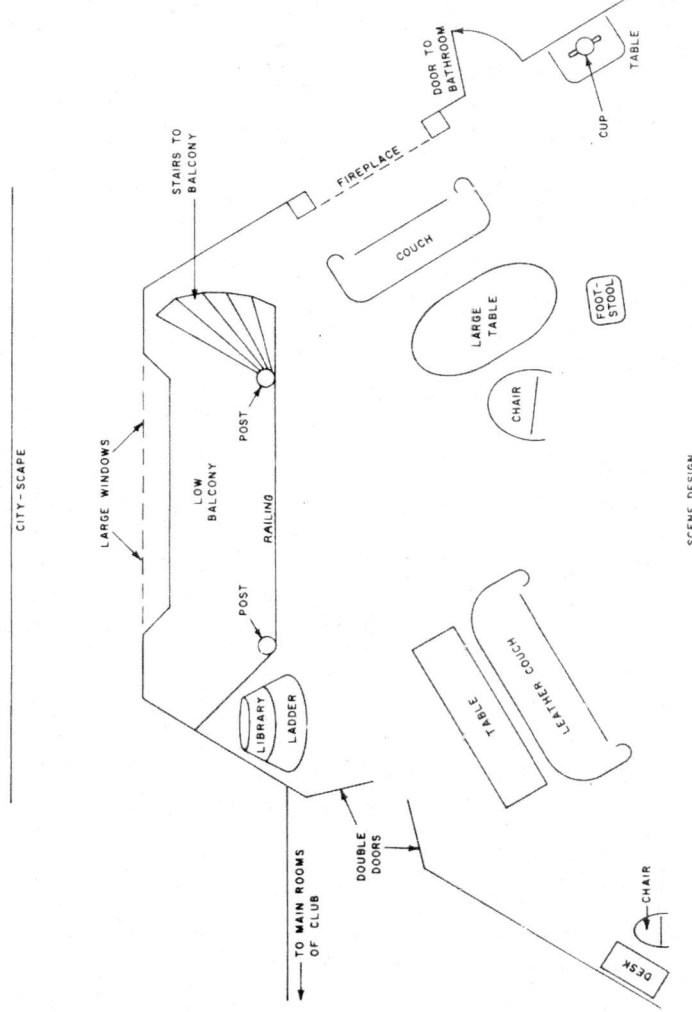

SCENE DESIGN

"THE MIDDLE AGES"

PROPERTY PLOT

ACT ONE

On Stage:
Bookcase, with books
Leather couches (2)
Desk, with chair
Large oaken tables (2) with trophies, prizes, magazines
Leather armchair
Shelves, with trophies and plaques
Assorted stuffed animal heads, guns (one loaded), fishing rods, polo
    mallets, portraits, tennis racquets, on walls and in racks
Small table, with silver cup on it
Library ladder
Footstool
Suitcase, by fireplace, with:
    Tablecloth
    Silver candlesticks
    Plates
    Toll House cookies
    Ice cream
    Smoked oysters
    Bottle of wine
    Matches
    Corkscrew
    Wine glasses

ACT TWO

Off Stage:
In bathroom:
    Bathrobe (Barney)
    Black negligée (Eleanor)
    Toilet brush
    Cap pistol
    "Bloody" towel

Off Stage:
Knitting bag (Eleanor)
Gin and tonic (Barney)
Wheelchair, with lap robe

Personal:
Watch (Barney)
Tape measure (Myra)

Personal:
Envelope, with deed, in pocket (Barney)
Purse, with compact (Myra)
Watch (Barney)

62